Jonathan Hand has over 20 years' experience as a practising barrister in Personal Injury and Clinical Negligence work. He has a particular specialism in equine and other animal related litigation, and is well-known for his expertise in this area. He is regularly instructed on behalf of both claimant and defendant clients in claims arising out of personal injury caused by animals, and he has also written and presented extensively on this topic. Jonathan is ranked by Chambers & Partners and by The Legal 500 as a leading junior in both Personal Injury and Clinical Negligence.

A Practical Guide to Personal Injury Claims Involving Animals

A Practical Guide to Personal Injury Claims Involving Animals

Jonathan Hand
Barrister
Outer Temple Chambers, London

Law Brief Publishing

Published 2017 by
Law Brief Publishing
30 The Parks
Minehead
Somerset
TA24 8BT

www.lawbriefpublishing.com

Paperback: 978-1-911035-15-2

To Jane Phillips

Who first started me on this road

Contents

CHAPTER ONE INTRODUCTION

Aim and scope of the book

As they have done for many centuries, animals play an important role in our daily lives. We may not encounter them directly every day, but we benefit from them in many ways, whether through sport or farming, as pets and companions, or as sources of interest and wonder in the wild. And when we do encounter them directly, in this country at least, our relationship with animals is generally harmonious.

But animals can, of course, be a danger, whether they are wild or tame. Indeed, it has been estimated that in this country animals are responsible for about 50,000 injuries each year.[1] It is no surprise then that disputes arise as a result of damage caused by animals, and that a body of law has developed which applies to such disputes. As explained below, this body of law is, in some respects at least, quite distinct. Lawyers and others involved with these disputes need therefore to have an understanding of the law in this field and of how it is applied in practice.[2] In particular, in claims involving personal injury caused by animals the liability aspects will often require some specialist knowledge which will not be acquired from other areas of personal injury litigation.

As the title says, this book deals with claims for personal injury caused by animals. It is intended to be a practical guide for those involved with litigation in this field.

A more detailed outline of the scope of the book, what it does and does not intend to cover, may also be helpful at the outset. It deals with liability for personal injury caused by animals, but not with claims arising out of other kinds of damage caused by animals, i.e. damage to property (including other animals and crops). Nor does it deal with the quanti-

1 See the report of the Pearson Commission (Report of the Royal Commission on Compensation for Personal Injury: Cmnd. 7054, 1978).

2 For a comprehensive account of the relevant law see *Civil Liability for Animals* by Sir Peter North (OUP, 2012), which is the principal work in this field.

fication of loss, once liability has been established.[3] It deals with the law in this area in England and Wales, although the law in other jurisdictions (including Scotland and Northern Ireland) is referred to where relevant. It deals with claims which can be brought in the civil courts of this jurisdiction. It should be borne in mind though that compensation for injury caused by animals may be recovered in other ways in certain circumstances. For example, claims by victims of violent crime under the Criminal Injuries Compensation Scheme where injury results from an animal attack[4] or for injury caused by animals as a result of low flying aircraft under the *ex gratia* compensation scheme operated by the Ministry of Defence. There is a wide range of legislation relating to animals which regulates their ownership and use, and which provides for criminal offences in connection with this (both for damage caused by animals, and for harm done to them).[5] But except to the extent that some of these statutes can be relevant to claims for damages for personal injury in the civil courts, consideration of this legislation also falls outside the scope of the book.

There is a now an extensive body of case law in this field, both in this jurisdiction and overseas. It would not fit with the purpose of the book as a practical guide to try to provide a comprehensive reference to all of the case law. Rather, the general approach is to identify the highest and most recent authority on the point in question, but with reference to other cases as well where they are thought to add something.[6] It should always be borne in mind, especially with the greater access to judgments

---

3 For the assessment of damages in personal injury claims, reference should be made to the specialist works which cover this field, such as *McGregor on Damages* and *Kemp and Kemp on the Quantum of Damages*.

4 See Annex B of the Criminal Injuries Compensation Scheme 2012, which provides that an animal attack in which the animal was used with intent to cause injury to a person amounts to a crime of violence so as to fall within the scope of the Scheme.

5 See, for example, the Dogs (Protection of Livestock) Act 1953, the Riding Establishments Act 1964, the Guard Dogs Act 1975, the Dangerous Wild Animals Act 1976, the Dangerous Dogs Act 1991, and the Animal Welfare Act 2006.

6 Only the neutral citation is given for those cases where this is available. For reported cases where there is no neutral citation, only the reference to the Official Law Reports is given where the judgment is reported in this series. For cases where the judgment has not been reported, the official transcript is often available through one of the online services, such as BAILLI, Westlaw or Lexis.

in all tribunals which is now available, that while first instance decisions may be interesting and useful, they are not authoritative decisions by an appellate tribunal; and that many decisions, even at appellate level, turn on their own particular facts, rather than establishing any general principle of law.

Claims to recover damages for personal injury caused by animals may conveniently be considered by reference to the two main grounds on which such liability can be founded, namely under the Animals Act 1971 and under the various common law causes of action. As explained in subsequent chapters, these two grounds are not mutually exclusive. Claims can be, and in practice often are, brought both under the Animals Act and in negligence and/or one of the other causes of action founded in common law. However, this distinction provides a helpful structure for the purpose of the book. It is divided into five main parts. The first three parts of the book deal with the Animals Act: Part 1 provides an introduction to the Animals Act; Part 2 deals with strict liability for dangerous animals; and Part 3 deals with the defences to strict liability for dangerous animals. The remaining two parts of the book deal with claims founded in common law: Part 4 concerns animals and the highway; and Part 5 deals with common law liability for animals generally.

The origins of the law imposing liability for harm done by animals stretches back to mediaeval times. A detailed account of the history of the law in this area, including the thinking behind the reform which led to the Animals Act 1971, is also outside the scope of this book.[7] But a summary of how the law has developed may be helpful by way of background, and to allow a better understanding of the present law as it applies to personal injury caused by animals which is covered in the remainder of the book.

---

7 See Chapter 1 of North, *Civil Liability for Animals* for such an account.

The background to the present law

A cause of action developed at common law for harm done by dangerous animals. It imposed strict liability (i.e. liability without proof of any fault) on the keeper of an animal for injury or other damage caused by the animal if either (i) the animal was classified as wild (*ferae naturae*), or (ii) the animal was not classified as wild, and so was considered tame (*mansuetae naturae*), but had a vicious propensity which was known to its keeper. This was known as the *scienter* action.[8] There was also a tort of cattle trespass for damage to property caused by straying livestock; and an exception to the general principles of negligence, which meant that an occupier of land adjoining a highway owed no duty of care to prevent his or her animals escaping onto the highway (known as the rule in *Searle v. Wallbank* [1947] A.C. 341, which was the final decision in the line of authority on this point). It was these features of the common law which were aptly described in the observation that: "*The law of torts has grown up historically in separate compartments and ... beasts have travelled in a compartment of their own.*"[9]

In addition to these special common law rules relating to harm done by animals there were also common law causes of action of general application, such as negligence, trespass to the person and nuisance, which could be relied on as well where harm was done by animals, albeit with some restrictions (such as the rule in *Searle v. Wallbank*, mentioned above). However, by the second half of the last century it was widely recognised that this branch of the law was unsatisfactory, and that it needed to be modernised and simplified. In 1953 a report recommending reform was produced by a committee chaired by Lord Goddard[10], and then in 1967 the Law Commission issued its Report on

---

8 Strictly speaking, it seems that the term *scienter* (meaning knowledge of wrongdoing) developed in relation to the claim for harm done by tame animals (for which proof of the keeper's knowledge of the animal's vicious tendency was required). But it is also used in relation to the claim for harm done by wild animals (perhaps on the basis that, in the case of wild animals, the keeper's knowledge of the animal's vicious tendency is irrefutably presumed).

9 Lord Simonds in *Read v. J. Lyons & Co. Ltd.* [1947] A.C. 156 at 182.

Civil Liability for Animals.[11] It was this latter report which led to the Animals Act 1971.

The Animals Act 1971 came into force on 1 October 1971. For convenience, it is often referred to simply as "the Act" in the remainder of the book. The full text of the Act in the form which is currently in force is reproduced in the Appendix to this book.[12] In the context of personal injury litigation, the Act brought about two main changes. First, it abolished the *scienter* action and the common law rules imposing strict liability for damage done by dangerous animals, replacing them with a new scheme of strict liability for such damage as set out in the Act; and, second, it abolished the rule in *Searle v. Wallbank*. There are various other provisions of the Act which do not impact on claims for personal injury (for example, the abolition of the common law liability for cattle trespass, and the new statutory rules dealing with straying animals) and which are therefore not considered further in this book.

An outline of the scheme of the Act relating to strict liability for damage done by dangerous animals is set out in the next chapter. There are though several other points relating to the Animals Act which can conveniently be mentioned here.

First, with the exception of the abolition of the rule in *Searle v. Wallbank*, the common law causes of action of general application mentioned above, including negligence, trespass to the person and nuisance, were not affected by the Act. It follows that the case law relating to these common law causes of action which preceded the coming into force of the Act may still be relevant today (with the exception of the

10 See the report of the Goddard Committee (Committee on the Law of Civil Liability for Damage done by Animals: Cmnd. 8746, 1953). The Goddard Committee recommended the abolition of strict liability for animals, and replacing this with liability for damage done by animals being based upon negligence. But this recommendation was not implemented; and, as we shall see, it was not followed by the Law Commission in its subsequent report.

11 Law Com. No. 13.

12 As at September 2017. The Act has most recently been amended by the Control of Horses Act 2015, although these changes (which relate to "fly-grazing" of horses) are not relevant to claims involving personal injury caused by animals.

decisions in the line of authority which culminated in *Searle v. Wallbank*). As noted already, these claims founded in common law are considered in the latter parts of the book, after the parts dealing with claims brought under the Act.

Second, the extent of the Animals Act is limited to England and Wales. In Northern Ireland the Animals (Northern Ireland) Order 1976[13] applies. This legislation contains provisions which are similar to those in the Act. In Scotland the Animals (Scotland) Act 1987 applies. This legislation adopted a somewhat different approach to the imposition of strict liability for damage caused by dangerous animals.[14]

Third, it should be borne in mind that the imposition of strict liability for damage done by dangerous animals is a matter of policy. It is essentially a question of where the risk of personal injury or other damage caused by dangerous animals should lie. The policy behind this part of the Act is that the risk should fall on someone who chooses to keep an animal and who can insure against it, as opposed to a member of the public who suffers damage caused by the animal. The approach was summed up in the Law Commission report which preceded the Act as follows: *"It does not seem unreasonable that the keeper of a dangerous animal should bear the special risk which is created by keeping it; moreover, it is a risk against which he can more conveniently insure than can the potential victim."*[15] As the House of Lords made clear in *Mirvahedy v. Henley* [2003] UKHL 16, that was a decision which was taken by Parliament when enacting the 1971 Act, and it is not for the Courts to form a view about the merits of the decision.[16]

Finally, there have been calls for, and various attempts at, reform of the Animals Act over the years. As we shall see in subsequent chapters dealing with the Act, it has been criticised for failing to provide the

13 SI 1976/1040.

14 See *Welsh v. Brady* [2009] CSIH 60 for a detailed account of the scheme of the Scottish legislation.

15 See §14 of the Law Commission Report on Civil Liability for Animals (Law Com. No. 13).

16 See *Mirvahedy* per Lord Nicholls at [6]; and see also per Lord Walker at [157].

simplification of the law in this area which it set out to achieve.[17] Instead, it is said that it has provided problems of interpretation and with that continuing uncertainty, in particular as a result of the wording of s.2(2) of the Act. There has also been concern about the policy behind the Act, as outlined above, and about the impact of the cost of insurance on those who keep animals, especially after the decision in *Mirvahedy* which appeared to widen the scope of strict liability. However, these attempts at reform have to date all run into the ground, and at the time of writing there do not appear to be any current substantive proposals for reform.[18]

17 As Lord Nicholls put it in *Mirvahedy* at [8]: *"The common law concerning liability for animals was notoriously intricate and complicated."* But Lord Walker went on to observe at [134] that whether the purpose of simplification was achieved by Parliament in the context of s.2(2) of the Act is *"far from clear"*.

18 See North, *Civil Liability for Animals* at paras. 2.92 to 2.96 for an account of the attempts at reform of s.2(2) of the Act following the House of Lords' decision in *Mirvahedy*.

PART ONE

INTRODUCTION TO THE ANIMALS ACT 1971

CHAPTER TWO
OUTLINE OF STRICT LIABILITY UNDER THE ANIMALS ACT

Liability for damage done by dangerous animals is imposed by s.2 of the Act. This includes liability for personal injury caused by animals of both a dangerous and non-dangerous species. As such, s.2 of the Act, and in particular sub-section 2, is the most important provision of the Act for the personal injury practitioner.

Liability is imposed by the Act on a keeper of the animal and is strict, in the sense that it does not require proof of any fault on the part of the keeper. Liability will attach if the relevant conditions prescribed by the Act are satisfied. This is, though, subject to the qualification that a keeper may nonetheless avoid liability if one of the defences provided by s.5 of the Act applies. The statutory defences are thus an important part of the scheme relating to strict liability under the Act.

This chapter provides an outline of strict liability for dangerous animals under the Act so far as it relates to personal injury claims. Chapter 3 covers various points of general application. The specific requirements of strict liability for damage caused by animals of a dangerous and a non-dangerous species and the defences to strict liability are then considered in turn in the chapters in Parts 2 and 3 respectively below.

It will be apparent that a claim based on strict liability under s.2 of the Act can succeed in circumstances where a fault-based claim such as a claim in negligence will not. However, this does not mean that a claim brought under s.2 is necessarily easier for a claimant to prove than a claim in negligence or the like. The need to devote the first three parts of this book to s.2 and the associated defences serves to illustrate the range of issues that can arise in the context of claims relating to strict liability for dangerous animals.

An outline of the scheme relating to strict liability for dangerous animals under the Act may be helpful at the outset. As explained in the previous chapter, under the old common law rules a distinction was made between liability for animals which were classified by law as "wild" and those which were "tame" (the two categories were referred to respectively as animals *ferae naturae* and *mansuetae naturae*). Although the old common law rules were abolished by s.1(1) of the Act, the distinction broadly remains in the Act. The Act distinguishes between animals belonging to a dangerous species and animals which do not (for convenience, this latter category is referred to as animals of a non-dangerous species).

Liability for damage caused by animals belonging to a dangerous species is dealt with in s.2(1) of the Act. Liability for damage caused by animals belonging to a non-dangerous species is dealt with in s.2(2) of the Act.

The Law Commission expressed its reasons for adopting this approach as follows:

> *"If, as we have recommended, there is to be a category of animals of a dangerous species for which strict liability is imposed, it would seem reasonable that an animal not belonging to that category should nevertheless give rise to strict liability in respect of injury or damage which it causes if that damage results from dangerous characteristics of the particular animal which are known to its keeper. As far as the potential defendant is concerned, he is equally the creator of a special risk if he knowingly keeps, for example, a savage Alsatian as if he keeps a tiger. As far as the potential plaintiff is concerned, an animal belonging to an ordinary harmless species, which is known to its keeper to be dangerous is in the nature of a trap – a "wolf in sheep's clothing" – which would seem to justify the same strictness of liability as applies to an obviously dangerous animal."*[1]

As we shall see in Part 2, the conditions prescribed by the Act for imposing strict liability differ as between these two sub-sections and hence between the category to which the particular animal belongs. Indeed, the courts have been concerned to preserve this distinction and to ensure that liability for an animal belonging to a non-dangerous

1 See para. 17 of the Law Commission Report on Civil Liability for Animals (Law Com. No. 13). As explained in Chapter 1 above, this report, which was published in 1967, was what led to the Animals Act subsequently being passed in 1971.

species is less strict than liability for an animal belonging to a dangerous species.[2]

Since all domesticated animals are classified as non-dangerous species (including horses, dogs and cows – the three species which feature most frequently in the case law), the vast majority of claims are brought under s.2(2) rather than s.2(1) of the Act. As Lord Walker put it in *Mirvahedy v. Henley* [2003] UKHL 16 at [135]:

> *"In practice section 2(1) has a very narrow scope, being almost entirely limited to incidents in (or following escapes from) zoos or circuses."*

Lord Walker went on to consider the wide range of situations in which, by contrast, claims under s.2(2) can arise:

> *"Section 2(2) has to cover the whole range of incidents involving animals of species classified as non-dangerous … . That range includes (i) physical injury to humans by biting (especially by dogs) or kicking or knocking down (especially by horses); (ii) injuries caused to livestock (such as a dog worrying a neighbour's sheep, or a cat killing a neighbour's chickens); (iii) road traffic accidents, especially those caused by animals straying on the highway; (iv) damage caused by livestock getting out on to neighbouring land and destroying crops or gardens; and (v) injury or damage caused by the spread of animal infection or by the smell or noise of animals (a class which shades off into cases normally classified as nuisance). So section 2(2) has a lot of work to do. It is expressed in general, abstract terms and it has to be applied to a wide range of disparate incidents."*[3]

Although s.2 is the main provision in the Act dealing with strict liability for dangerous animals, there are a number of other relevant provisions. These are s.5, which contains the statutory defences mentioned already; s.6, which deals with the interpretation of certain expressions used in both s.2 and s.5, including the important definition of a keeper; and the

2 See *Turnbull v. Warrener* [2012] EWCA Civ 412, in particular at [4] per Maurice Kay L.J. and at [37] per Stanley Burnton L.J..

3 *Mirvahedy* at [135].

general provisions about interpretation of the Act in s.11. The provisions of the latter two sections are addressed where relevant in the next chapter and elsewhere (as indicated, the statutory defences are dealt with separately in Part 3).

CHAPTER THREE GENERAL PRINCIPLES AND DEFINITIONS

(i) MEANING OF ANIMAL AND SPECIES

There is no general definition of an animal in the Act. The Act does though define "livestock" and "poultry", and the creatures listed within these definitions would seem to be considered animals.[1] North suggests that the term "animal" should include birds, reptiles, and insects, but not bacteria and similar organisms.[2]

The species of an animal is relevant both to the question of whether it belongs to a dangerous species for the purpose of s.2(1)[3] and (if it does not) of whether it has characteristics not normally found in animals of the same species for the purpose of s.2(2)(b).

The Act provides in s.11 that "species" includes sub-species and variety.

The meaning of species has been considered in a number of cases involving dogs in the context of s.2(2)(b). Paragraph (b) requires a comparison to be made between the characteristics of the animal which has caused the damage and of animals of the same species. In *Hunt v. Wallis* [1994] P.I.Q.R. 128 a Border Collie called Bruce had run into the claimant, causing her to fall and injure herself. The question arose as to whether the comparison required by paragraph (b) should be between the dog and dogs generally or the dog and the breed of dog concerned. Pill J. answered this question as follows:

---

1 See s.11 of the Act for the definition of "livestock" and "poultry". This section also provides that a horse includes an ass, mule or hinny.

2 North, *Civil Liability for Animals* at para. 2.04. In *Kane v. McKenna* (1991) 1 B.N.I.L. 105 a bantam cockerel, which had seriously injured a child (and had apparently previously killed a goat) was held to be an animal, to which the Animals (Northern Ireland) Order 1976 (equivalent to the Animals Act 1971 in that jurisdiction) applied.

3 The question of whether an animal belongs to a dangerous species is considered in the next chapter dealing with liability under s.2(1) of the Act.

> *"The comparison for the purpose of paragraph (b) is, in my judgment, between Bruce and the characteristic Border Collie. Where there is an identifiable breed of dog, a breed of long standing with acknowledged and identifiable characteristics, at least where it is a breed whose qualities are recognised as beneficial to man, the comparison should be with that breed or sub-species."*

His approach was thus that s.2(2)(b) should be determined by reference to the characteristics of the breed of dog involved, at least where such a comparison can sensibly be made. He was thereby equating breed with variety or sub-species as referred to in s.11. The same approach has been taken in cases involving other breeds of dog, including Alsatians[4], Rottweilers[5], and Bull mastiffs[6].

However, it would seem that a claimant can choose to frame his or her case so that the comparison is made either with the breed of dog in question or with dogs as a species. Certainly this was the approach taken in *Preskey v. Sutcliffe* (18 February 2013, Leeds County Court: unreported), where the claimant had been bitten by a Boxer whilst trying to restrain it. The judge found that there was no evidence that the dog had characteristics not normally found in a Boxer; but it was accepted that in certain circumstances all dogs may bite, including when they feel territorially challenged, and on that basis s.2(2)(b) was satisfied.

It might be argued that a similar approach should be taken in cases involving other animals, so that the comparison can be made with the breed of animal in question. For example, in the case of horses, a comparison might be made with thoroughbreds, which are said to have

---

4 *Cummings v. Granger* [1977] Q.B. 397, *Gloster v. Chief Constable of Greater Manchester* [2000] P.I.Q.R. 114, and *Dhesi v. Chief Constable of the West Midlands* [2000] Po.L.R. 120. In *Cummings*, where the Alsatian was used as a guard dog, Ormrod L.J. observed that it would be wrong to treat a guard dog as being a variety of a species or a sub-species for the purpose of s.2(2) (and hence the appropriate comparison was with Alsatians as a breed and not with guard dogs).

5 *Chauhan v. Paul* (19 February 1998, Court of Appeal: unreported).

6 *Curtis v. Betts* [1990] 1 W.L.R. 459.

particular characteristics, being quicker and sharper with faster reactions than some other breeds.

It appears that the meaning of species has not yet been considered in the context of s.2(1). As North points out, there is no logical basis for taking a different approach to the interpretation of this term as between the two sub-sections. Hence it is suggested that the same approach outlined above in the context of s.2(2)(b) should also be followed in the context of s.2(1).[7]

(ii) WHO IS A KEEPER?

The statutory definition

As mentioned in the last chapter, liability for a dangerous animal under s.2 of the Act is imposed on a keeper of the animal. In order to identify the potential defendant (or defendants) to a claim it is therefore necessary to identify the keeper (or keepers) of the animal at the relevant time.

The question of who is a keeper of an animal is governed by s.6(3) and s.6(4) of the Act, which provide as follows:

> *(3) Subject to subsection (4) of this section, a person is a keeper of an animal if–*
>
> *(a) he owns the animal or has it in his possession; or*
>
> *(b) he is the head of a household of which a member under the age of sixteen owns the animal or has it in his possession;*
>
> *and if at any time an animal ceases to be owned by or to be in the possession of a person, any person who immediately before that time was a keeper thereof by virtue of the preceding provisions of this subsection continues to be a keeper of the animal until another person becomes a keeper thereof by virtue of those provisions.*

7 See North, *Civil Liability for Animals* at para. 2.10.

> *(4) Where an animal is taken into and kept in possession for the purpose of preventing it from causing damage or of restoring it to its owner, a person is not a keeper of it by virtue only of that possession.*

It follows that a person[8] can be a keeper in a number of different ways. Specifically, as (i) the owner of the animal, (ii) someone who has the animal in his or her possession, or where a child under age sixteen owns or possesses the animal, (iii) the head of the household of which that child is a member.

Animals can of course be abandoned or escape. Where this happens, the Act provides that an original keeper (i.e. a person who was a keeper before the animal was abandoned or escaped) remains liable until another person takes over ownership or possession.

An exception is provided by s.6(4) in the case of a person who takes and keeps possession of an animal in order to prevent it from causing damage or to restore it to its owner. In this situation the person in possession of the animal is not treated as its keeper. So if the animal then causes damage whilst in that person's possession, he or she cannot be liable for that damage under the Act.

There are a number of features of this definition of a keeper which can be important in practice.

No need for possession

First, it is clear that a person can be liable as the owner even if the animal is not in his or her possession at the relevant time. Thus lack of control over the animal (see below about the meaning of possession) does not permit an owner to avoid liability, since he or she will remain a keeper.[9] Conversely, a person with possession of an animal can be liable even though he or she does not also own it.

---

8 Schedule 1 to the Interpretation Act 1978 provides that "person" includes a body of persons corporate or unincorporate. It follows that liability under the Act may attach to an individual, a company, a partnership, and an unincorporated association.

9 See *Collings v. Home Office* [2006] C.L.Y. 160.

What amounts to possession

Second, since a person can be liable as a result of his or her possession of an animal, the question of what amounts to possession can be important. Under the old common law rules a person had possession of an animal where he or she had some control of it. There is no reason to think that the Act has changed things in this regard, and so the cases decided under the common law may be referred to should there be a dispute about whether or not someone has possession.[10]

On this basis, in relation to horses, it would seem that the proprietor of a livery stables or training yard would have control of the horses at the stables/yard so as to be a keeper. By contrast, it has been held that a landowner who allowed a horse onto its land under a grazing agreement was not in possession of the animal at the relevant time and so was not a keeper (presumably on the basis that the grazing agreement did not confer any control over the animal on the landowner).[11]

Multiple keepers

Third, more than one person can be a keeper at the relevant time, i.e. where the animal is in the possession of someone other than the owner. Thus a claimant may be faced with having to decide whether or not to pursue more than one defendant when bringing a claim under s.2. The usual considerations about claims against multiple defendants apply in this situation, including the risk on costs if a claim succeeds against one defendant but fails against another and the ability of each defendant to meet any judgment. In a claim involving an animal of a non-dangerous species, it is also important to bear in mind the requirement to prove knowledge on the part of a keeper (or those whose knowledge is imputed to a keeper) under s.2(2)(c) of the Act. Knowledge of the relevant characteristics of the animal (or lack of it) may differ between keepers. This needs to be considered carefully at the outset, as it can

---

10 See North, *Civil Liability for Animals* at paras. 2.12 to 2.15 which contain a helpful commentary on the common law on this aspect and the cases decided under it.

11 *Doolan v. EP Cornall & Sons* [2001] C.L.Y. 324.

often be the way that a claimant may be able to prove knowledge on the part of one keeper but not another.

One keeper may want to bring a claim against another. In *Flack v. Hudson* [2001] Q.B. 698 the court had to decide whether such a claim could be made under the Act. The facts of the case are worth reciting. Mrs Flack was exercising a horse owned by Mrs Hudson. The horse had a propensity to take fright when it came upon agricultural machinery. The trial judge found that this was known to Mrs Hudson but not to Mrs Flack. As Mrs Flack was riding the horse along a road they came upon a tractor and sprayer. The horse took fright and bolted. Mrs Flack fell off and suffered fatal injuries. The trial judge found that Mrs Flack was a keeper of the horse at the relevant time, and that there was no bar to a claim being made against Mrs Hudson as the owner of the horse and another keeper. The Court of Appeal upheld the decision that a person in possession of an animal who is not its owner (i.e. a bailee) can claim against the owner, since:

> *"At common law (absent knowledge of the defect on the part of the bailee) the bailee has a clear and well established cause of action. There is nothing in the [Animals] Act which expressly or by implication deprives the bailee of his cause of action or which limits the persons who can sue a keeper (i.e. owner or bailee) to third parties and strangers. If it had been the intention of Parliament to deny the right, it would have expressly provided for this to happen."* [12]

<u>*Contribution*</u>

Finally, since more than one keeper may be liable to a claimant under the Act, a keeper may look to recover a contribution from another keeper in respect of that liability under the Civil Liability (Contribution) Act 1978. It is important to have this point in mind when acting for a defendant keeper, so that a claim for a contribution is made

12 Per Otton L.J. at [17]. The absence of a bar against one keeper suing another under s.2 of the Act would appear not to be limited just to a claim by a bailee against an owner: see in particular Keene L.J. in *Flack* at [44]-[45]. A cross-appeal against the finding that Mrs Flack was a keeper at the relevant time, on the basis that she was "merely a transient rider", was also dismissed.

against another keeper where appropriate. But bear in mind as well the point made above, that in a claim involving an animal of a non-dangerous species, knowledge of the relevant characteristics of the animal (or lack of it) may differ between keepers. Thus it may be that the other keeper would not have been liable to the claimant for the same damage under s.2(2), and so a claim for a contribution based on the other keeper being liable as well under the Act would not succeed. As to apportionment, the usual principles would apply, although it is difficult to see how an assessment of the relative blameworthiness can be made between two keepers in a case involving strict (i.e. no fault) liability alone.[13] As North puts it, it may well be that in many cases of liability under s.2 apportionment will be equal.[14]

(iii) DAMAGE

Liability under s.2 of the Act is imposed for damage caused by an animal. Causation is considered below, but it is worth noting first several points in relation to the damage for which a claimant can recover under s.2.

"Damage" is defined by s.11 of the Act as including the death of, or any injury to, any person (including any disease and any impairment of physical or mental condition). Thus a claimant can recover for personal injury of any kind, and where a person is killed by an animal the estate and dependants of the deceased can recover damages arising from the death.[15]

---

13 By s.2(1) of the Civil Liability (Contribution) Act 1978 the amount of the contribution shall be such as may be found by the court to be just and equitable having regard to the extent of that person's responsibility for the damage in question. In making its assessment of the contribution in this way a court must have regard both to the blameworthiness of the parties and their contribution to the damage in question. For a case in which a contribution between two keepers of an animal featured, and the relevance on apportionment of whether a claim in negligence was also made out against one of the keepers, see *Hole v. Ross-Skinner* [2003] EWCA Civ 774.

14 See North, *Civil Liability for Animals* at para. 2.31.

Although s.11 only refers to death and personal injury, it seems clear (since this is not an exclusive definition) that damage to property caused by an animal is also recoverable under s.2, where the requirements of strict liability are satisfied. Thus a claim may be brought to recover for property damage, including injury to another animal: for example, where a horse collides with and damages a vehicle, or where a dog attacks and injures another dog.

In a claim involving damage by an animal of a non-dangerous species the second limb of s.2(2)(a) requires the damage to be of a kind which, if caused by the animal, was likely to be severe. The test relates to the likelihood of the animal causing the relevant damage. It is not a requirement that a claimant must in fact have suffered severe damage in order to recover under s.2(2).

(iv) CAUSATION

Under both s.2(1) and s.2(2) of the Act liability is imposed for damage which is "caused by an animal".

It appears to be generally accepted that strict liability under s.2 requires proof of direct causation only, and that there is no requirement of reasonable foreseeability of the damage.[16]

In cases involving animals of a non-dangerous species, there is though the additional requirement that the damage must be caused by the dangerous characteristics relied on for the purpose of s.2(2) (as well as

---

15 S.10 of the Act provides that for the purposes of the Fatal Accidents Acts 1846 to 1959 any damage for which a person is liable under s.2 of the Act shall be treated as due to his fault. By Schedule 1 of the Fatal Accidents Act 1976, which was passed subsequent to the Animals Act, the reference in s.10 of the Animals Act to the previous Fatal Accidents Acts includes reference to the Fatal Accidents Act 1976.

16 Although there appears to be no reported case on this point, see the commentary on causation under s.2 of the Act in *Clerk & Lindsell on Torts (21st Ed.)* at para. 21-03 (footnote 14), and in North, *Civil Liability for Animals* at paras. 2.60 and 2.75. But cf. *Winfield & Jolowicz on Tort (19th Ed.)* at para.17-027.

the requirement about the likelihood of the animal causing the relevant damage under s.2(2)(a), which is dealt with in Chapter 6).[17]

The case law provides some guidance about the approach to causation under the Act, and where the courts are likely to draw the line between what is or is not considered to be a direct consequence of an animal's conduct. In short, it seems that in the large majority of cases this aspect of causation (i.e. proof that the damage was caused by the animal) will not be a difficult hurdle for a claimant to overcome.

In *Chauhan v. Paul* (19 February 1998, Court of Appeal: unreported), a postman was injured when he fell over as a result of being chased down the drive by a large Rottweiler (notwithstanding that the dog in question was described by the trial judge as "a big softie"). The claim under the Act failed both at trial and on appeal, as the requirements of s.2(2) were not made out on the facts. But Wall J. in the Court of Appeal also made some helpful (albeit *obiter*) comments on causation:

> *"In my judgment, whether or not the injury was "caused by" the animal is essentially an issue of fact. Thus, to take one of the examples canvassed in argument, if an innocuous dog barks at me as I am walking along the pavement and as a result I jump into the path of an approaching car, it may well be that any injuries I suffer were not caused by the dog, but by my excessive reaction to the dog's bark. ... However, if I am approached at speed by a large dog whose intentions may (unbeknown to me) be friendly; if as a consequence I take the reasonable decision to remove myself from the scene as soon as possible; and if in the process of running away I am chased by the dog and injure myself by falling over or having a heart attack, on these facts the damage I suffer is, in my judgment, caused by the dog."*

In another dog case, *Smith v. Ainger* (The Times, 5 June 1990: Court of Appeal), the defendants' dog went to attack the claimant's dog, and in doing so struck the claimant's legs, knocking the claimant to the

17 The question raised in *Turnbull v. Warrener* [2012] EWCA Civ 412 about whether a claimant who is injured in an "ordinary riding accident" after losing control of a horse and falling off suffers "damage caused by" the horse is dealt with in Chapter 5.

ground, as a result of which he was injured. As the trial judge put it: *"the attack was an attack by dog on dog, to which the plaintiff's accident was incidental."* Although the main issue on appeal to the Court of Appeal was whether s.2(2)(a) was satisfied on the facts, it appears to have been accepted that causation was properly made out in these circumstances, i.e. even where the injury was "incidental" to the conduct of the animal.

The question of causation is also relevant in the context of the statutory defence under s.5(1) of the Act. This defence provides that a keeper is not liable under s.2 for any damage which is due wholly to the fault of the person suffering it. Thus in a case where a defendant seeks to rely on this statutory defence, a court will have to decide whether or not the cause of the claimant's damage was solely the fault of the claimant (if it was partly due to the negligence of the claimant and partly due to the conduct of the animal, then primary liability can be made out but with a deduction from the claimant's damages for contributory negligence).[18]

As mentioned already, in cases involving animals of a non-dangerous species, there is the additional requirement that the damage must be caused by the dangerous characteristics relied on for the purpose of s.2(2). This was made clear by the Court of Appeal in *Curtis v. Betts* [1990] 1 W.L.R. 459.[19]

The need for a claimant to prove a causal connection between the characteristic in question and the damage suffered is well-illustrated by the decision in *Mirvahedy v. Henley* [2003] UKHL 16. The facts of *Mirvahedy* are set out in more detail in Chapter 7; but, in summary, three horses kept by the defendants escaped from their field after being frightened during the night and got on to a main road, where one of them collided with the claimant's car, as a result of which he suffered serious injuries. The claim failed on causation at first instance, because the trial judge found that the accident was not caused by the relevant characteristics (a frightened horse's propensity to bolt, to continue to

18 See further the discussion of the statutory defence under s.5(1) in Chapter 10.

19 See in particular per Stuart-Smith L.J. at page 470. See also *McKenny v. Foster* [2008] EWCA Civ 173 per May L.J. at [33].

flee, and to ignore obstacles in its path) but rather by the horse's mere presence on the road. In this respect, the trial judge relied on an earlier decision of the Court of Appeal in *Jaundrill v. Gillett* (The Times, 30 January 1996). This finding on causation was overturned by the Court of Appeal, who placed particular reliance on the evidence that the horses were still behaving abnormally once they reached the main road and that it was this behaviour which caused the accident. In view of this, the requirement that the dangerous characteristics had caused the damage suffered by the claimant had been made out.[20]

In some cases it may be readily apparent that the characteristics of the animal relied on by the claimant are what caused the damage. But in other cases the position may not be so straightforward, and in these cases it will be important to address this aspect in the evidence (as *Mirvahedy* demonstrates). For example, using the factual situation in *Mirvahedy* of one or more horses escaping on to a road and colliding with a car, the questions of whether there was something abnormal about the horse(s) behaviour on the road and of whether this led to the collision and consequent damage will need to be investigated. If a claimant cannot establish these elements of causation then a claim under the Act will not succeed.

For completeness (although this issue may be an unlikely one to encounter in practice), it may be noted that in cases involving damage caused by an animal of a dangerous species under s.2(1) it appears that there is no requirement for the damage to be related to the characteristics which caused its species to be classified as dangerous under s.6(2)(b). This was the position under the old common law rules, and the Act appears to leave the position unchanged (hence the reference in s.2(1) to liability for "any damage" caused by an animal).[21]

20 *Mirvahedy v. Henley*, in particular per Lady Hale at [16]. The Court of Appeal's decision on causation was upheld on the appeal to the House of Lords (see in particular per Lord Walker at [161] to [163]). It has been suggested that on the facts, and following the decision in *Mirvahedy*, it is likely that the claimant in the earlier case of *Jaundrill v. Gillett* would today succeed on causation (as he had done before the trial judge): see *Charlesworth & Percy on Negligence (13th Ed.)* at para. 14-41 (footnote 116).

21 See North, *Civil Liability for Animals* at paras. 2.55 and 2.56. North cites the decision in *Behrens v. Bertram Mills Circus Behrens* [1957] 2 Q.B. 1, a case under the old common law rules relating to animals of a dangerous species (animals *ferae naturae*), in which Devlin J. gave these examples to illustrate the point: *"If a person wakes up in the middle of the night and finds an escaping tiger on top of his bed and suffers a heart attack, it would be nothing to the point that the intentions of the tiger were quite amiable. If a tiger is let loose in a funfair, it seems to me to be irrelevant whether a person is injured as a result of a direct attack or because on seeing it he runs away and falls over."* See also *Tutin v. Mary Chipperfield Promotions Ltd* (1980) 130 N.L.J. 807 discussed in Chapter 4 below.

PART TWO

STRICT LIABILITY FOR DANGEROUS ANIMALS UNDER THE ANIMALS ACT 1971

CHAPTER FOUR
LIABILITY FOR ANIMALS OF A DANGEROUS SPECIES: S.2(1) ANIMALS ACT

Introduction

As explained in Chapter 2, liability for damage done by dangerous animals is imposed by s.2 of the Act. In this context, the Act distinguishes between animals belonging to a dangerous species and animals which do not (for convenience, this latter category is again referred to as animals of a non-dangerous species). Liability for damage caused by animals belonging to a dangerous species is dealt with in s.2(1) of the Act, while liability for damage caused by animals of a non-dangerous species is dealt with in s.2(2).

The conditions prescribed by the Act for imposing strict liability differ as between these two sub-sections. This chapter looks at the specific requirements for strict liability for animals of a dangerous species under s.2(1) (the requirements for strict liability for animals of a non-dangerous species are dealt with in the following chapters of Part 2). It also looks at what is a dangerous species.

As also mentioned in Chapter 2, in practice the vast majority of claims involve damage caused by animals which belong to a non-dangerous species and are thus brought under s.2(2). Claims involving animals of a dangerous species do though arise from time to time, as the case law in this context (albeit limited) demonstrates.

The question of whether a particular animal is or is not of a dangerous species is plainly an important one, since it determines which of the two sub-sections (with their differing requirements for strict liability) applies. The question needs therefore to be considered at the outset in any case, even though in most cases the answer will be obvious and uncontentious.

What is a dangerous species?

By s.6(2) of the Act a "dangerous species" is defined as follows:

> *A dangerous species is a species –*
>
> *(a) which is not commonly domesticated in the British Islands; and*
>
> *(b) whose fully grown animals normally have such characteristics that they are likely, unless restrained, to cause severe damage or that any damage they may cause is likely to be severe.*

There are thus two conditions that must both be satisfied for a species to be classified as dangerous under the Act.

Not commonly domesticated

First, as provided by s.6(2)(a), it must be a species which is not commonly domesticated in the British Islands. By reference to the verb "domesticate", it has been suggested that the meaning which is most appropriate in this context is "to tame or bring under control". So species of animals which are commonly tamed or brought under control in this country cannot belong to a dangerous species.[1]

Importantly, this means that strict liability for commonly domesticated animals is dealt with by s.2(2) and not by s.2(1). This covers horses, dogs (save, possibly, certain "fighting" breeds: see below), and cows (including bulls), and also cats and chickens (including cockerels, as in *Kane v. McKenna* (1991) 1 B.N.I.L. 105), all of which are considered commonly domesticated in the British Islands.

The use of the word "commonly" in s.6(2)(a) seems to be intended to catch those species which are domesticated in this country but only relatively infrequently (either in absolute numbers or where the majority of the species live in the wild in this country). On this basis, it would seem likely that monkeys and snakes, for example, would be held to be not commonly domesticated.

1 See Lord Scott in *Mirvahedy v. Henley* [2003] UKHL 16 at [87].

Dangerous characteristics

The second condition, as provided by s.6(2)(b), is to determine whether the species is dangerous. The wording is similar to the test for whether an animal of a non-dangerous species is to be considered dangerous under s.2(2)(a) of the Act. There are two limbs to this second condition, either of which may be satisfied: a *"double-barrelled concept of dangerousness with alternative criteria either of which suffices"*, as Lord Hobhouse put it in *Mirvahedy v. Henley* [2003] UKHL 16 at [67]. Lord Hobhouse went on to give examples of how each of these criteria of dangerousness would be satisfied, as follows:

> *"Using the first alternative, a tiger is a dangerous animal. It is likely, unless restrained, to cause severe injuries to humans: that is its nature. Using the second alternative, an Indian elephant is a dangerous animal, not because it is likely to injure any one, but because, if it does, the injury is likely, as a result of its weight and bulk, to be severe: cf Behrens v. Bertram Mills Circus Ltd [1957] 2 Q.B. 1. This is a statement about its physical capacity to injure and its inability to limit the consequences of that capacity not about its inclination to injure."*

It seems clear that, as with the old common law distinction between animals *ferae naturae* and *mansuetae naturae*, the question of whether or not a particular species of animal meets the conditions for a dangerous species as provided by the Act is a question of law. It is a matter for the judge based on common knowledge about animals (i.e. a matter of judicial notice). Although a court might admit some evidence about the nature of a particular species, it would not be determinative of the issue.[2] Further, since this is a question of law, previous decisions about whether or not a particular species is dangerous are binding, subject to the conventional principles of precedent.

However, because of the relative infrequency of claims under s.2(1), the reported decisions on this issue are very limited. It has been held that a camel is a dangerous species within the meaning of the Act.[3] North also

2 See *Charlesworth & Percy on Negligence (13th Ed.)* at para. 14-09, and *Behrens v. Bertram Mills Circus Ltd* [1957] 2 Q.B. 1 at pages 15-16.

gives a helpful list of species which may be expected to be classified as dangerous, including bears, lions, tigers, wolves, and elephants.[4] The Dangerous Wild Animals Act 1976 regulates the keeping of such animals and contains in Schedule 1 a list of animals to which that Act applies. It seems that an animal which is named in Schedule 1 of the 1976 would be considered an animal of a dangerous species for the purpose of s.6(2).[5]

Further, the fact that the particular animal which caused the damage may be tame is irrelevant. As the wording of s.6(2) makes clear, the test depends on the nature of the species to which it belongs and not on the nature of the particular animal.

Strict liability under s.2(1) of the Act

Unlike the wording of s.2(2) (discussed in the next chapter), the wording of s.2(1) of the Act is straightforward:

> *(1) Where any damage is caused by an animal which belongs to a dangerous species, any person who is a keeper of the animal is liable for the damage, except as otherwise provided by this Act.*

So if an animal which has caused damage is held to belong to a dangerous species, its keeper (or keepers) will be liable under s.2(1) of the Act without more, subject only to whether the keeper can rely on one of the statutory defences. In particular, by contrast with s.2(2), a claimant is not required to prove a keeper's knowledge of the animal's dangerous characteristics.

The nature of strict liability under s.2(1) was explained by Lord Nicholls in *Mirvahedy* at [13], as follows:

---

3 *Tutin v. Mary Chipperfield Promotions Ltd* (1980) 130 N.L.J. 807, discussed below.

4 North, *Civil Liability for Animals* at para. 2.46.

5 See *Clerk & Lindsell on Torts (21st Ed.)* at para. 21-02. See also the reference there to the Dangerous Dogs Act 1991, and that it may be argued that the specified breeds of dangerous dog (certain "fighting" breeds from overseas) in the 1991 Act also fall within the scope of s.2(1) of the Act.

> *"If you choose to keep a dangerous animal not commonly domesticated in this country, you are liable for damage done by the animal. It matters not that you take every precaution to prevent the animal escaping. You may not realise that the animal is dangerous. Liability is independent of fault. Liability is independent of knowledge of the animal's dangerous characteristics. You are liable, subject only to certain defences of general application set out in section 5."*

One of the very few reported decisions involving s.2(1) of the Act is *Tutin v. Mary Chipperfield Promotions Ltd* (1980) 130 N.L.J. 807. The claim was brought by Dorothy Tutin, the actress, following a fall from a camel at a charity event in which she was taking part at Olympia. This involved a camel race with various celebrity riders, during which she was unseated by the ungainly movement of the camel and fell to the ground injuring her spine. The judge held that a camel was a dangerous species since (a) it was not commonly domesticated in the British Islands (even though it is found as a domesticated animal in many other parts of the world), and (b) it was conceded that camels may cause severe damage by biting or kicking, even though their characteristics are not such that they are likely to cause such damage unless restrained (and so the second limb of s.6(2)(b) was satisfied). The requirements for liability under s.2(1) were therefore made out, even though the cause of Miss Tutin's injury was simply the movement of the camel whilst she was riding it, as opposed to anything in the form of an attack such as a bite or a kick. This illustrates the point made about causation in the previous chapter, that in a claim involving an animal of a dangerous species it is not necessary for the damage to be related to the characteristics which caused its species to be classified as dangerous.

CHAPTER FIVE
LIABILITY FOR ANIMALS OF A NON-DANGEROUS SPECIES: S.2(2) ANIMALS ACT – INTRODUCTION

The wording of s.2(2)

As explained in previous chapters, liability for damage caused by animals of a non-dangerous species is imposed by s.2(2) of the Act. As also mentioned, in practice the vast majority of claims involve damage caused by animals which belong to a non-dangerous species and are thus brought under s.2(2) (the question of whether or not an animal belongs to a dangerous species is dealt with in the previous chapter). Hence it is this provision of the Act which is by far the most important for personal injury practitioners dealing with claims involving animals.

Unfortunately, the wording of s.2(2) is far from straightforward. It has attracted much judicial criticism over the years. In the two most recent Court of Appeal cases involving s.2(2), the drafting of the sub-section has been described as "oracular and opaque" and "grotesque".[1] As a result, it has caused particular problems of interpretation and application (and continues to do so), with consequent difficulty and uncertainty for lawyers and their clients; and it has produced an extensive body of case law since the Act came into force over 45 years ago, including the House of Lords' decision in *Mirvahedy v. Henley* [2003] UKHL 16 and numerous decisions in the Court of Appeal.

The full text of s.2(2) of the Act is as follows:

> *(2) Where damage is caused by an animal which does not belong to a dangerous species, a keeper of the animal is liable for the damage, except as otherwise provided by this Act, if–*

1 See respectively Jackson L.J. in *Goldsmith v. Patchcott* [2012] EWCA Civ 183 at [31] and Maurice Kay L.J. in *Turnbull v. Warrener* [2012] EWCA Civ 412 at [4].

(a) the damage is of a kind which the animal, unless restrained, was likely to cause or which, if caused by the animal, was likely to be severe; and

(b) the likelihood of the damage or of its being severe was due to characteristics of the animal which are not normally found in animals of the same species or are not normally so found except at particular times or in particular circumstances; and

(c) those characteristics were known to that keeper or were at any time known to a person who at that time had charge of the animal as keeper's servant or, where that keeper is the head of a were known to another keeper of the animal who is a member of that household and under the age of sixteen.

There are thus three separate requirements of strict liability for an animal of a non-dangerous species, as set out in paragraphs (a), (b) and (c) respectively of s.2(2). In order to establish liability on this basis, a claimant must satisfy the requirements of each of these three paragraphs. As was said in *Smith v. Ainger* (The Times, 5 June 1990: Court of Appeal), it is important that the court should consider paragraphs (a), (b) and (c) of s.2(2) in turn and that the trial judge should make the necessary findings of fact so that it is clear on what basis, if any, liability is established.[2]

For the same reason, the three paragraphs also provide an essential checklist for lawyers when bringing or defending a claim under s.2(2). Each of these paragraphs, and the specific requirements for strict liability which they each impose, are considered in turn in the following chapters of this part.

---

2 The judgment of Neill L.J. in *Smith v. Ainger* contains a detailed and helpful "checklist" which sets out the steps that should be considered where a claim is brought under s.2(2) (see pages 5 to 8 of the transcript of the judgment in *Smith*).

Scope of strict liability under s.2(2)

There is though a general point about the scope of strict liability under the sub-section which may conveniently be dealt with at this stage.

As mentioned in Chapter 2, the courts have been concerned about whether there is a distinction in practice between s.2(1) and s.2(2). In general terms, this concern about a "lack of content" in s.2(2) has recently led to a greater emphasis being placed on whether the knowledge requirement in paragraph (c) can be satisfied, as well as on the statutory defences, especially the defence of voluntary acceptance of risk under s.5(2) of the Act.[3] It would be dangerous though for claimants to assume from these judicial observations that the requirements of s.2(2), and in particular those in paragraphs (a) and (b), can easily be satisfied in any case of this kind. As the case law reviewed in the following chapters makes clear, establishing each of the requirements of s.2(2) is not always a straightforward task, and many cases have foundered on one or more of these statutory obstacles.

In the context of riding cases, this concern has also led to some of the judges in the Court of Appeal in *Turnbull v. Warrener* [2012] EWCA Civ 412 questioning whether what was described as "an ordinary riding accident" falls within the scope of s.2(2) at all.[4] A distinction was drawn between an accident such as occurred in that case, where a rider lost control of a horse and fell off (i.e. an ordinary riding accident)[5], and

---

3 See *Mirvahedy v. Henley* (in particular Lord Nicholls in at [43]), *Goldsmith v. Patchcott* [2012] EWCA Civ 183 (in particular Jackson L.J. at [33] and [40]-[41]) and *Turnbull v. Warrener* [2012] EWCA Civ 412 (in particular Maurice Kay L.J. at [4] and Stanley Burnton L.J. at [37]).

4 See Lewison L.J. at [43]-[49], with whom Stanley Burnton L.J. expressly agreed. Lewison L.J. referred to the Law Commission's report on Civil Liability for Animals, from which the Animals Act 1971 was derived; and specifically the old common law rules, which the Law Commission considered limited liability to an act of the animal which was in the nature of an "attack", and from which the Law Commission did not intend the proposed legislation to depart.

5 Lewison L.J. referred to *Welsh v. Stokes* [2007] EWCA Civ 796 (where the claimant's horse reared up, causing her to fall onto road) and *Freeman v. Higher Park Farm* [2008] EWCA Civ 1185 (where the claimant's horse bucked as she went into canter, causing her to fall off) as examples of other cases involving an ordinary riding accident.

cases where the injury resulted from an attack by the animal (for example, a kick or a bite from a horse). It was questioned whether a rider who is injured in an accident of the former kind suffers "damage caused by" the horse, and hence whether such a case is covered by s.2(2). If it is, then Lewison L.J. considered that the Act *"has caused a major (and unintended) expansion in the potential scope of strict liability"*. In the event, the appeal in *Turnbull* was determined on other grounds, and the Court of Appeal did not decide this issue, so it remains to be argued on another day in cases involving accidents of this kind.[6]

6 See *Kublin v. Jane Allison Equestrian Ltd* (30 April 2013, Oxford County Court: unreported). The claimant was injured in what the judge accepted was an ordinary riding accident when her horse spooked and slipped, trapping her leg as it fell on top of her. The judge concluded however that, in circumstances where the horse had fallen on to the rider causing her injury, it would be difficult to say that the damage was not "caused by" the horse.

CHAPTER SIX
LIKELIHOOD OF THE KIND OF DAMAGE: S.2(2)(A) ANIMALS ACT

Introduction

The purpose of paragraph (a) of s.2(2) is to determine whether the animal in question is a dangerous animal (even though of a non-dangerous species) because of its abnormal characteristics, as identified in paragraph (b).

The wording of paragraph (a) provides for a "double-barrelled" concept of dangerousness, in the same way as the definition of a dangerous species in s.6(2) (as considered in Chapter 4 above in relation to claims under s.2(1) of the Act). There are thus two separate limbs of paragraph (a); and it is sufficient for a claimant to satisfy either of the two limbs in order to succeed under the paragraph.[1]

The questions that need to be answered under paragraph (a) may be put as follows:

- Is the damage of a kind which the animal, unless restrained, was likely to cause? [first limb]
- If the animal caused this kind of damage, was it likely to be severe? [second limb][2]

As the wording makes clear, the questions need to be answered by reference to the animal concerned and the damage it has caused.

In the two most recent Court of Appeal cases involving s.2(2), the court appeared to give rather mixed messages about paragraph (a). Specific-

---

1 It appears though that the two limbs should not be considered mutually exclusive: in *Smith v. Ainger*, for example, it was held that the claimant had made out both limbs of paragraph (a).

2 See the questions as expressed by Maurice Kay L.J. in *Turnbull v. Warrener* [2012] EWCA Civ 412 at [10] with some amendment.

ally, in *Goldsmith v. Patchcott* [2012] EWCA Civ 183 Jackson L.J. said at [33] that:

> *"It can be seen that sub-section (2)(a) catches two types of damage. First, there is damage which the animal is likely to cause, if the animal is not restrained. Secondly, there is damage which the animal is unlikely to cause, but which is likely to be severe if the animal does cause it.* ***It should be noted that [paragraph (a)] will only eliminate a small number of cases. Most animal-related damage which someone wishes to sue about will fall into one or other of those two categories."*** [emphasis added]

The brief facts in *Goldsmith* were that the claimant was injured when the horse she was riding reared up and bucked violently. She was thrown to the ground and then struck by the horse's hoof. It was not disputed that on these facts paragraph (a) was satisfied. It should be borne in mind that Jackson L.J.'s observations about paragraph (a), whilst they may clearly be expected to carry weight with a trial judge, were therefore *obiter*.

Just over a month later, in *Turnbull v. Warrener* [2012] EWCA Civ 412, two of the judges in a differently constituted Court of Appeal took a rather different approach. They upheld the trial judge's decision that the second limb of paragraph (a) had not been made out on the evidence (there was no challenge to the judge's finding that the first limb of paragraph (a) had not been established). This was in another riding case, on broadly similar facts, where the claimant was injured when she lost control of a horse she was riding with a bitless bridle. The horse took off at speed and she fell from the horse, landing on a tarmac road.

So where does that leave things at present? It is probably safe to say that claimants must still expect to have to show that paragraph (a) is satisfied (unless of course this is conceded by a defendant), and that a court is likely to be prepared to take evidence on the point (more on this below).

How should the questions under paragraph (a) be framed?

It has been pointed out in a number of cases that the questions relating to each limb of paragraph (a) need to be answered by reference to the circumstances of the individual case. As Neill L.J. put it in *Smith v. Ainger* (The Times, 5 June 1990: Court of Appeal):

> *"It also seems clear that the likelihood of damage or of its being severe has to be considered in the circumstances of the particular case."*

For example, in *Bodey v. Hall* [2011] EWHC 2162 (QB), the claimant was travelling as a passenger in a pony and trap when the pony bolted and the trap tipped over, causing her to be thrown out and suffer a severe head injury. The judge held that the questions needed to be considered by reference to a person being thrown from or out of a moving trap when the horse had shot forwards expectedly.[3]

However, as was pointed out in *Turnbull*, the answer to the question can depend on the way in which the question itself is framed, and the generality (or otherwise) of the reference to the accident circumstances. Lewison L.J. explained the point as follows at [51] (by reference to the facts in the earlier case of *Welsh v. Stokes* [2007] EWCA Civ 796):

> *"The problem, as I see it, is the level of generality at which you ask and answer the question. If the question is: if you fall off a rearing horse onto a hard surface, and the horse falls on top of you, is the injury likely to be severe, you may get one answer. But if the question is: if you fall off a horse is the injury likely to be severe, you may get another. I do not believe that this problem has yet been squarely confronted in the cases."*[4]

This is another aspect where some further guidance from the courts might be helpful. For the time being, claimants need to consider care-

---

3 See the judgment in *Bodey* at [31]-[33], which contains a summary of the relevant dicta on this point in previous cases. The judge held that in these circumstances the injury was likely to be severe, and so the second limb of paragraph (b) was satisfied.

4 See also Lord Scott in *Mirvahedy* at [101] who made a similar point about how specifically (or otherwise) the "kind" of damage is defined for the purpose of paragraph (a) by reference to the circumstances of the individual case.

fully how they formulate their case under paragraph (a), including the questions put to expert witnesses where appropriate; and defendants need in turn need to consider carefully how to respond to the way in which the case is put, and whether a different formulation of the relevant question(s) should be advanced.

Terminology

Before looking at each of the two limbs of paragraph (a) in more detail, some points also need to be made about the terminology used in this paragraph.

As explained in Chapter 3, "damage" is defined in s.11 of the Act as including death and personal injury, including any disease and any impairment of physical or mental condition. So, the "kind" of damage as referred to in paragraph (a) would seem to contemplate (for example) personal injury, or perhaps something more specific such as physical injury, disease etc.[5]

Both limbs of paragraph (a) require consideration of the "likelihood" of damage. Indeed, paragraph (a) can be said in this way to be concerned with the foreseeability of the damage that an animal may cause.[6] The meaning of "likely" has been considered in a number of cases, with reference to the level of expectation that is required. In *Smith v. Ainger* Neill L.J. said that a probability of damage was not required and that it included an event "such as might happen" or "such as might well happen". This was considered at some length by Lord Scott in *Mirvahedy v. Henley* [2003] UKHL 16 at [95]-[97], who preferred to use the meaning "to be reasonably expected" (although he acknowledged that there may be no material difference between this and Neill L.J.'s phrase "such as might well happen"). Lord Scott added that "a mere possib-

5 In *Smith v. Ainger* the kind of damage was identified even more specifically, by reference to the particular circumstances in which the injury had been sustained by the claimant, as *"personal injury to a human being caused by the direct application of force"*. See also Lord Scott's comments in *Mirvahedy* at [101] about defining the "kind" of damage referred to above.

6 See *Curtis v. Betts* [1990] 1 W.L.R. 459 per Stuart-Smith L.J. at page 469.

ility" was not enough. Although Lord Scott's comments on this point were *obiter*, it seems to be generally accepted now that "likely" should be given the meaning which he proposed of "reasonably to be expected".[7] But if this semantic debate about the level of expectation required is settled at more than a possibility but less than a probability, applying such relatively fine calibration in practice remains at times a challenge.

The first limb of paragraph (a)

Turning to the first limb of paragraph (a), Lord Phillips in *Clark v. Bowlt* [2006] EWCA Civ 978 at [14] expressed the requirement of this limb as follows:

> *"The keeper of a domestic animal can only be liable under the first limb of s.2(2)(a) if it has caused damage in circumstances where, unless tethered, it was likely to cause that damage."*

So this limb will only be satisfied in the case of an animal which, if it escapes from control (i.e. it is not restrained, or is not "tethered" to use Lord Phillips' language), is reasonably to be expected to cause damage of the kind suffered by the claimant.

Smith v. Ainger illustrates how the first limb may be satisfied in practice. The facts in *Smith* were that the defendants' dog, Sam, went to attack the claimant's dog as they passed each other on the pavement. In doing so, Sam struck the claimant's legs, knocking the claimant to the ground, as a result of which he was injured. There was evidence from the dog register at the local police station of two previous incidents where Sam had attacked another dog, and on each of these occasion the owner of the other dog had suffered bites in trying to separate the two dogs. The trial judge had found that Sam had a propensity to attack other dogs, but not humans, and so concluded that paragraph (a) was not satisfied. The Court of Appeal took a different view and held that, in view of his history including the injuries suffered by the owner of the other dog as a

7 See for example Etherton L.J. in *Freeman v. Higher Park Farm* [2008] EWCA Civ 1185 at [33] and Maurice Kay L.J. in *Turnbull v. Warrener* at [12].

result of the attack, unless restrained Sam was likely to cause damage of this kind in the situation which arose (i.e. personal injury due to the direct application of force), and so the first limb of paragraph (a) was satisfied.[8]

The evidence about previous incidents where the animal had caused injury as a result of the same characteristics was plainly key to the claim succeeding on this issue on appeal in *Smith*. So too in another dog case, *Kite v. Napp* (The Times, 1 June 1982), where the defendant's Irish Wolfhound had attacked the claimant, who was carrying a bag. There was evidence that this dog had previously attacked people carrying bags on two other occasions. It was held that the first limb of paragraph (a) (as well as the second limb of the paragraph) was made out.

But what of the situation where a dog is off the lead and runs into or jumps up and knocks someone over, causing them to fall and suffer injury, without any suggestion of an attack (whether on a human or another animal)? It has been held that in this situation the dog was unlikely to cause physical injury, and so the first limb was not satisfied.[9] Importantly, there was a finding in each case that the dog did not have a propensity to collide with or jump up at people.

There is also some uncertainty about the effect of the words "unless restrained" in the first limb of paragraph (a). It is sometimes argued by defendants that the animal in question was in fact restrained at the relevant time, and hence that the first limb of paragraph (a) cannot be satisfied. This argument succeeded in *Kublin v. Jane Allison Equestrian Ltd* (30 April 2013, Oxford County Court: unreported), where the judge held that the rider had regained some control of the horse after it

8 As mentioned already, the Court of Appeal held that the second limb of paragraph (a) was also satisfied (see also below). But see, by contrast, *Gloster v. Chief Constable of Greater Manchester Police* [2000] P.I.Q.R. P114, where it was held that a trained Police dog was not likely to cause damage unrestrained in the particular circumstances of that case, and so the first limb of paragraph (a) was not made out.

9 See *Hunt v. Wallis* [1994] P.I.Q.R. 128 and *Whippey v. Jones* [2009] EWCA Civ 452. In *Hunt* the judge went on to find (with some misgivings) that in view of the Court of Appeal's decisions in dog cases relating to the second limb of paragraph (a) (see *Cummings v. Grainger* [1977] Q.B. 397, *Curtis v. Betts* and *Smith v. Ainger*), the second limb of paragraph (a) was made out in that case.

had tried to take off, such that the animal was restrained at the time when it subsequently fell and injured her; and on that basis the first limb of paragraph (a) did not apply.[10] This argument can in turn lead to debate about whether or not on the facts an animal was restrained at the relevant time, as well as about what exactly is required for an animal to be restrained.

The second limb of paragraph (a)

As to the second limb of paragraph (a), this requires an assessment of the likelihood of any damage of the kind in question which is caused by the animal being severe.

The case of *Cummings v. Granger* [1977] Q.B. 397, one of the earliest reported cases under the Act, illustrates how the second limb may be satisfied in practice. This is the case, in Lord Denning's words, of the barmaid who was badly bitten by a big dog. The dog in question was an Alsatian, which was used to guard a scrap yard in East London next to the pub where the claimant worked. The claimant went into the yard after work one night and was attacked by the dog. She was badly bitten on the face. Lord Denning upheld the trial judge's decision that paragraph (a) was made out, since: *"this animal was a dog of the Alsatian breed; if it did bite anyone, the damage was 'likely to be severe.'"*

This approach to the second limb of paragraph (a) has been followed in subsequent cases involving dogs, both where the damage has been caused by a bite[11] and also by a collision.[12]

---

10 See the judgment in *Kublin* at [53]. But see also *Hughes v. Rosser* (2008, Swansea County Court: unreported) at [91] where it appears that an argument by the defendant to this effect was rejected.

11 See, for example, *Curtis v. Betts*, *Dhesi v. Chief Constable of the West Midlands* [2000] Po.L.R. 120, and *Preskey v. Sutcliffe* (18 February 2013, Leeds County Court: unreported).

12 See *Smith v. Ainger* and *Hunt v. Wallis*.

So too in a number of cases involving horses, where the injury has been caused by biting[13] and also by a kick[14].

But what of the not-uncommon situation, as occurred in *Mirvahedy v. Henley*, where one or more animals get on to a road and collide with a vehicle? Paragraph (a) was not in issue on the appeal in *Mirvahedy*, as it had been conceded by the defendant that it was satisfied. But, as mentioned already, Lord Scott nonetheless considered this paragraph at some length in his speech in *Mirvahedy*. Although *obiter* (and although he was in the minority on the appeal) his comments about paragraph (a) may clearly be expected to carry considerable weight. In particular, Lord Scott made the point at [96] that the question under the second limb of paragraph (a): *"cannot be answered by simply referring to the seriousness of the damage actually caused in the case in question. To do so would be to ignore the inclusion … of the word 'likely'."*[15] He then went on to consider whether paragraph (a) was made out on the facts of the case and doubted whether it was, saying this at [98]:

> *"My own impression, however, is that a horse loose on the highway does not actually result in damage to third parties, that if damage to third parties does result the damage is not usually severe, no more, perhaps, than a dent to a car, and that the cases in which serious injury or damage results are fortunately few and far between."*

So it remains open to a court in a case involving similar facts to those in *Mirvahedy* to find that the requirements of the second limb of paragraph (a) (or indeed the first) are not made out.[16]

---

13 See *Whitehead v. Alexander* [2000] C.L.Y. 205 and *Tapp v. Trustees of the Blue Cross Society* (15 May 2013, Northampton County Court: unreported).

14 See *Breeden v. Lampard* (21 March 1985, Court of Appeal: unreported), *Millward v. Pritchard* (1 March 2007, Llangefni County Court), *Smith v. Harding* (26 November 2013, Manchester County Court: unreported).

15 See also *Turnbull v. Warrener* per Lewison L.J. at [51]. It would also seem to follow that it is not necessary for the damage suffered by the claimant in fact to be severe in order to satisfy the second limb of paragraph (a), only that any damage caused by the animal was likely to be so: see *Charlesworth & Percy on Negligence (13th Ed.)* at para. 14-42, and North, *Civil Liability for Animals* at para. 2.69.

16 It should though be noted that Lord Slynn in *Mirvahedy* observed at [52] that in his view paragraph (a) had been correctly conceded, since it was likely that the

The case law indicates that claims arising out of riding accidents can also give rise to controversy in relation to the second limb of paragraph (a). Shortly after *Mirvahedy* was decided, it was argued successfully by the defendant in *Elliott v. Townfoot Stables* [2004] C.L.Y. 169, in reliance on Lord Scott's *obiter* comments in *Mirvahedy*, that paragraph (a) was not satisfied. This was a case involving a young child who was unseated during a riding lesson when her pony made a sudden movement (described by the judge as *"not a real buck but ... a sudden and unbalancing movement or series or quick movements that caused [the claimant] to fall."*). She injured her shoulder, fracturing her upper humerus. The judge concluded that in these circumstances (severe) damage was a mere possibility but was not reasonably to be expected.

Then in *Welsh v. Stokes* [2007] EWCA Civ 796 it was held that the second limb of paragraph (a) was satisfied, in circumstances where a horse had reared up, causing the claimant to fall on to the road, and the horse itself had then fallen backwards on to her (the trial judge's decision on this point was not challenged on the appeal, and indeed was endorsed by the Court of Appeal).[17] The approach in *Welsh* was expressly followed by the Court of Appeal in another riding accident case, *Freeman v. High Park Farm* [2008] EWCA Civ 1185, in which the claimant had again fallen from her horse, on this occasion when it had bucked as it went to canter. Etherton L.J. expressed the court's reasoning as follows at [34]:

> *"It is obvious that, if a horse bucks on beginning to canter so that the rider falls off, it is reasonably to be expected that severe injury will result. In Welsh v. Stokes at para [40] Dyson LJ ... regarded this as*

---

damage if caused would be severe (i.e. that the second limb of paragraph (a) was satisfied). See also Lord Hobhouse at [68]. The other two members of the House of Lords, Lord Nicholls and Lord Walker, did not express a view about paragraph (a). See also *McKenny v. Foster* [2008] EWCA Civ 173, in which a driver was injured and her passenger killed when their car collided with a cow which had escaped on to the road. The trial judge held that the criteria of paragraph (a) were fulfilled. Although these findings were challenged by the defendant on appeal, the Court of Appeal did not find it necessary to deal with this issue (the appeal was determined by reference to paragraph (b), as discussed below).

17 See Dyson L.J. at [40] (with whose judgment the other two members of the Court of Appeal agreed).

> *self-evident in the case of a rider falling from a horse who rears. I see no reason why the same approach should not be appropriate in the case of a rider falling from a bucking horse about to canter."*

It seems it was this approach which informed the comments of Jackson L.J. about paragraph (a), quoted above, in the Court of Appeal's subsequent decision in *Goldsmith v. Patchcott.*

But, as already mentioned, in *Turnbull v. Warrener*, the most recent case involving s.2(2) in the context of a riding accident to come before the Court of Appeal, the majority of the court took a markedly different approach. Rather than this being a question which had essentially been resolved by the previous cases, they thought it was a live issue which fell to be decided on the evidence in the individual case. The trial judge's finding that the second limb of paragraph (a) was not satisfied, which was based on evidence from the claimant's equine expert when cross-examined, was upheld. As Lewison L.J. put it:

> *"I do not, with respect, regard it as self-evident that a rider who falls off a rearing horse (or for that matter a cantering horse) is likely to suffer severe injury. It has not been suggested that the expert evidence on the likelihood of injury was inadmissible, even though Etherton L.J. [in Freeman v. Higher Park Farm] suggested that expert evidence need not be called. In my judgment the judge was entitled to rely on that evidence and make the finding of fact that he did."* [18]

So it seems clear following *Turnbull* that, in riding accident cases at least, a claimant would be well-advised to adduce some evidence to prove the second limb of paragraph (a) where this is relied on; and a defendant will likewise need to consider whether there is evidence to challenge this.[19]

---

18 At [54]. See also Stanley Burnton L.J. at [39] to the same effect. Maurice Kay L.J., by contrast, considered that the trial judge's decision on this issue could not be upheld as it ran contrary to the decisions in the previous cases, and in any event was not supported by the evidence which the judge had relied on.

19 In *Turnbull* the question of the approach to determining paragraph (a) was determinative of the appeal in relation to s.2(2)(a). By contrast, in the previous Court of Appeal cases mentioned above paragraph (a) was either not a live issue on the appeal (see *Welsh* and *Goldsmith*) or the question of the approach to determ-

There is a practical difficulty here, however. There is little in the way of statistical evidence to assist on the issue, certainly so far as riding accidents are concerned (and indeed the use of such evidence was deprecated by the Court of Appeal in *Freeman*).[20] Equine and other experts can be asked to address the issue, but (in the absence of any helpful statistics) their opinion must inevitably be one of impression, and impressions can vary. It is primarily for this reason that the question of whether the second limb of paragraph (a) is satisfied remains a contentious issue in some cases, with the outcome depending very much on the particular facts and the evidence before the court in each individual case.[21]

---

ining paragraph (a) did not fall to be considered (see *Freeman*). Thus the approach endorsed by the majority of the Court of Appeal in *Turnbull* should be binding on a lower court. Further, although in *Turnbull* only the second limb of paragraph (a) was in issue on the appeal (the first limb of paragraph (a) had been found not to be satisfied at trial, and this was not challenged on the appeal), it would seem to follow that the same approach should equally be applied in relation to the first limb of paragraph (a). See also in this regard *Lynch v. Ed Walker Racing Ltd* (15 June 2017, QBD: unreported).

20 See Etherton L.J. at [40] (although this was before the different approach indicated by the majority of the Court of Appeal in *Turnbull*, as just outlined).

21 See, for example, *Kublin v. Jane Allison Equestrian Ltd*, where it was held that on the evidence, and in particular the expert evidence, it could not be said that any injury was likely to be severe in the circumstances in which the claimant came to fall from her horse.

CHAPTER SEVEN CHARACTERISTICS OF THE ANIMAL: S.2(2)(B) ANIMALS ACT

Introduction

Paragraph (b) of s.2(2) is concerned with the source of the animal's dangerousness.[1] The essential requirement of paragraph (b) is that the animal in question has a characteristic which is abnormal for its species. However, although the essential requirement of paragraph (b) is defined by reference to the abnormality of the characteristic, this should not be taken as suggesting that paragraph (b) will only be satisfied in unusual or rare cases. Indeed, one of the concerns expressed by the courts in relation to paragraph (b) is about whether it contains any content, and hence whether it operates to restrict the scope of strict liability under s.2(2) in any way. This, and the rather convoluted wording of the paragraph, explains why paragraph (b) features so prominently in the case law.

The opening words of paragraph (b) provide that: *"The likelihood of the damage or of its being severe was due to characteristics of the animal ..."*. This refers back to the requirement under paragraph (a) relating to whether the animal in question is a dangerous animal. The characteristics which satisfy paragraph (b) must be what make the animal dangerous for the purpose of paragraph (a). In this way there is a link between paragraph (a) and paragraph (b). This is an important aspect of the overall statutory framework for strict liability under s.2(2) and is considered further below.

It is now well-established, following the House of Lords' decision in *Mirvahedy v. Henley* [2003] UKHL 2003, that there are two separate limbs to paragraph (b), and that it is sufficient for a claimant to satisfy one or other of these two limbs. The requirements under these two limbs are truly alternative, in the sense that only one or other can be satisfied.

1 See Lord Nicholls in *Mirvahedy* at [16].

It is also well-established that there must be a causal link between the characteristics which satisfy paragraph (b) and the damage suffered by the claimant.[2] Thus the enquiry in relation to paragraph (b) must focus on the characteristics which the animal manifested at the time when the injury or other damage was suffered by the claimant.

The questions that need to be answered under paragraph (b) may therefore be put as follows:

- Was the damage suffered by the claimant caused by characteristics of the animal which are not normally found in animals of the same species? [first limb] – alternatively

- Was the damage suffered by the claimant caused by characteristics of the animal which are not normally found in animals of the same species except at particular times or in particular circumstances? [second limb]

Mirvahedy v. Henley

Until the House of Lords' decision in *Mirvahedy* there were two different interpretations of the wording of paragraph (b), which could make the difference between whether or not strict liability was established. One approach, which was referred to in *Mirvahedy* as the *Cummings* interpretation (after the approach adopted in *Cummings v. Granger* [1977] Q.B. 397 and followed in *Curtis v. Betts* [1990] 1 W.L.R. 459), favoured a literal and wider interpretation. As Lord Nicholls put it in *Mirvahedy* at [5], this approach allowed for strict liability to be imposed: *"for damage caused by the animal when the animal's behaviour in the circumstances was in no way abnormal for an animal of the species in those circumstances"*. It is this approach which was favoured by the majority of the House of Lords in *Mirvahedy*. On this approach there are two separate and alternative limbs of paragraph (b), as described above. The other approach, which was referred to in *Mirva-*

2 See *McKenny v. Foster* [2008] EWCA Civ 173 per May L.J. at [33] (and the references to the earlier cases cited in that paragraph). See also the section on causation in Chapter 3 above.

hedy as the *Breeden* interpretation (after the approach adopted in *Breeden v. Lampard* (21 March 1985, Court of Appeal: unreported) and followed in *Gloster v. Chief Constable of Greater Manchester Police* [2000] P.I.Q.R. 114), favoured a purposive and narrower interpretation. This approach excluded the situation such as arose in *Mirvahedy* (i.e. where damage was caused by an animal behaving perfectly normally for its species in the particular circumstances) from the scope of strict liability.

Although the wider, *Cummings* interpretation was upheld by a majority of only three to two of their Lordships in *Mirvahedy*, there has been no subsequent attempt to find a way around it in the courts and it seems the approach can now be regarded as well-established. It is not necessary therefore to go any further into the detail of the competing arguments relating to paragraph (b) which were considered in *Mirvahedy*.[3]

It is though worth noting the concern expressed in *Mirvahedy* by Lord Nicholls, who ultimately favoured the wider *Cummings* interpretation, that this interpretation seems to leave paragraph (b) with very limited content. Lord Nicholls said at [43]:

> *"Thus the Cummings interpretation means that requirement (b) will be met in most cases where damage was caused by dangerous behaviour as described in requirement (a). Requirement (b) will be satisfied whenever the animal's conduct was <u>not</u> characteristic of the species in the particular circumstances. Requirement (b) will also be satisfied when the animal's behaviour <u>was</u> characteristic of the species in those circumstances."*

It was this point which led Jackson L.J. to observe subsequently in *Goldsmith v. Patchcott* [2012] EWCA Civ 183 at [40] that: *"it is not obvious, to me at least, what purpose section 2(2)(b) serves."* This was

3 A detailed commentary on the competing arguments in *Mirvahedy* and the different opinions of the House of the Lords on this issue may be found in North, *Civil Liability for Animals* at paras. 2.78 to 2.83. The cases before *Mirvahedy* which had applied the alternative *Breeden* interpretation (in particular *Breeden v. Lampard* itself and *Gloster v. Chief Constable of Greater Manchester Police*), which was rejected by the majority of the House of Lords in *Mirvahedy*, should not now be followed so far as they relate to the application of paragraph (b).

echoed shortly afterwards by Maurice Kay L.J. in *Turnbull v. Warrener* [2012] EWCA Civ 412 who said at [18] that *"the approach by which we are bound is very favourable to a claimant"* and at [22] that *"the drafting of s.2(2)(b) has resulted in its virtual emasculation."*

However, it would be unwise to deduce from these judicial comments that paragraph (b) will rarely, if ever, prove contentious. While *Mirvahedy* has undoubtedly provided helpful clarification of the law in this area, there remain several aspects relating to paragraph (b) which can present practical difficulties for a claimant, and opportunities for a defendant seeking to avoid liability. Before turning to look at these further aspects, it may be helpful first to see how the two separate limbs of paragraph (b) may be satisfied in practice.

The first limb of paragraph (b)

Flack v. Hudson [2001] Q.B. 698 illustrates how the first limb may be satisfied. The facts in *Flack* are set out in Chapter 3 above, but are repeated here for convenience. Mrs Flack was exercising a horse owned by Mrs Hudson. The horse had a propensity to take fright when it came upon agricultural machinery. The trial judge found that this characteristic was known to Mrs Hudson but not to Mrs Flack. In particular, there had been an incident about 18 months before the accident involving Mrs Flack when the horse had bolted on coming across a large tractor. The accident involving Mrs Flack occurred when she was riding the horse along a road and came upon a tractor and sprayer. The horse took fright and bolted. Mrs Flack came off the horse on to the road and was killed. The trial judge accepted the expert evidence that it was not a normal characteristic for horses to bolt in these circumstances. He found that it was an abnormal characteristic for horses to behave in this way when coming across agricultural machinery and as such this horse had a characteristic which satisfied the first limb of paragraph (b). The trial judge's finding on this aspect was upheld on appeal.

The second limb of paragraph (b)

Mirvahedy itself illustrates how the second limb may be satisfied. In *Mirvahedy* three horses kept by the defendants escaped from their field at night. Something had frightened them very badly, although it was never established what it was. The horses broke through both an electric fence and the surrounding wooden fence. They then fled for about 300 yards down a track and for almost a mile down a minor road before reaching a main road, where one of them collided with the claimant's car, landing on its roof. The claimant suffered serious injuries as a result of the collision. There was evidence that they were behaving in a way that showed they were still frightened when they got on to the road, and that it was this behaviour which caused the accident. Horses are not normally in a mindless state of panic, nor do they normally ignore obstacles in their path. So this was not normal behaviour for horses in general. But it was accepted that it is perfectly normal for horses to behave in this way (i.e. to bolt, continue to flee, and ignore obstacles in their path) in circumstances where they are frightened. As such, as explained above, the second limb of paragraph (b) was held to be satisfied, based on the interpretation favoured by the majority of the House of Lords.[4]

Evidence

The importance of carefully identifying the characteristics relied on for the purpose of paragraph (b) will no doubt be apparent from the commentary above. In practice, it will often be necessary for claimants to obtain expert evidence both to assist in formulating the claim and then to prove it, if liability is disputed. Indeed, instructing an appropriate expert at an early stage of the claim will often pay dividends for both claimants and defendants. Not only will it assist in assessing the

4 As mentioned already, in *Mirvahedy* the majority approved the approach taken in two previous cases involving dogs where it was held that the second limb of paragraph (b) was satisfied, namely *Cummings v. Granger* (attack in circumstances where the dog was used as a guard dog) and *Curtis v. Betts* (attack in circumstances where the dog was defending what it regarded as its territory). But see the below on the link between paragraphs (a) and (b) as to the relevant characteristics relied on in these two previous cases.

merits, but it should allow the claim or defence to be set out in a way that shows it has been properly investigated in the correspondence under the pre-action Protocol (a letter of claim that simply sets out the wording of s.2(2) without more, as is sometimes seen, rather suggests the opposite). It should also ensure that a consistent case can then be advanced in any subsequent statements of case, if proceedings are issued. It is not, of course, for an expert to advise on whether or not the requirements of s.2(2) are satisfied. But a good expert, properly instructed, should be able to advise in particular on the characteristics which the animal manifested at the time when the injury or other damage was suffered, and in turn on whether these characteristics are abnormal by reference to the two limbs of paragraph (b).

The danger of failing to adduce evidence to establish the requirement of paragraph (b) is demonstrated by *Freeman v. Higher Park Farm* [2008] EWCA Civ 1185. The claimant was riding a horse provided by the defendant riding centre. There was evidence that the horse had a habit of bucking when going into canter. On the day in question the horse had bucked when starting to canter on two occasions. On the second occasion the claimant fell off and was injured. The trial judge concluded that neither limb of paragraph (b) was satisfied on the evidence, and this was upheld by the Court of Appeal, albeit for somewhat different reasons. In particular, the Court of Appeal referred to the absence of any expert or other evidence about the bucking of horses in general or when going into canter. One cannot help thinking that the outcome might well have been different if the court had had the benefit of evidence going to these points.

What is a characteristic?

The question of what amounts to a characteristic for the purpose of paragraph (b) is not just a sterile exercise in semantics. If a court concludes that the actions of the animal relied on by a claimant cannot properly be described as a characteristic then the claim is likely to fail on this basis alone. The term is not defined by the Act.

In *Fox v. Kohn* (2 November 1995, Court of Appeal: unreported) Otton L.J. considered the meaning of a characteristic in this context and referred to the definition in the Shorter Oxford English Dictionary of *"a distinctive mark, a distinguishing peculiarity or quality"*. He also referred to an animal having *"a propensity, a proclivity, a tendency, which does distinguish it from its fellows of the species"*.

It seems that a characteristic may be either innate (i.e. due to the inherent character of the animal) or learnt (i.e. due to the animal's training or other experiences).[5]

Lord Walker considered the meaning of the term at some length in *Mirvahedy* at [138]-[139]. This passage contains some helpful guidance, in particular since it gives several pointers to what amounts to a characteristic for the purpose of each of the two limbs of paragraph (b):

> *"It must refer to character or disposition as evinced by overt behaviour – for instance, a dog which had the habit of attacking people who were carrying bags: Kite v. Napp … : all dangerous characteristics are likely to be more or less permanent but they may show themselves either frequently and randomly (as with the unreliable horse in Wallace v. Newton …), or under a stimulus peculiar to the particular animal (such as bag-carrying in Kite v. Napp), or under some internal or external stimulus (such as the animal's hormones or a perceived challenge to its territory) which can be expected to produce similar behaviour in most animals of its species. … I consider that Mr Sharp (for the respondent) must be right in suggesting that predictability (of how animals of the same species react to a particular stimulus or situation) is one of the indicia of characteristic behaviour which falls within the second limb of section 2(2)(b)."*

Clark v. Bowlt [2006] EWCA Civ 978 also sheds some light on what does, or does not, amount to a characteristic. The claimant was injured when a horse moved suddenly into the path of his passing car in a movement that could not be controlled by its rider. The trial judge

5 See *Gloster v. Chief Constable of Greater Manchester Police* per Hale L.J. at page 120.

identified the relevant characteristic as "a propensity occasionally to move otherwise than as directed". Lord Phillips in the Court of Appeal doubted whether this could be described as a characteristic of an animal. It seems that the objection was directed at the lack of any distinct behavioural quality being identified: a horse (or any other animal) may move in a way that cannot be controlled, and contrary to the direction being given, for any number of reasons.

It is not necessary, however, for the characteristic to be a "vicious" one, in the sense that it shows a tendency for the animal to injure people by attacking them. This is shown by the case of *Wallace v. Newton* [1982] 1 W.L.R. 375, referred to in the passage from Lord Walker's speech in *Mirvahedy* quoted above, in which the claimant was injured whilst handling a horse named (with nice irony) Lord Justice. Lord Justice was found to be unpredictable and unreliable in his behaviour, in a way that is not normally found in a horse, such that the first limb of paragraph (b) was satisfied. It was accepted that this unpredictability and unreliability in his behaviour amounted to a dangerous characteristic, even though it could not be said that the horse had a vicious tendency to injure people.[6]

In claims based on the second limb of paragraph (b), there is a further potential difficulty for claimants since it is necessary to show a degree of predictability of the behaviour relied on at the particular time or in the particular circumstances. This point arose in *Turnbull v. Warrener* [2012] EWCA Civ 412. The claimant was injured when the defendant's horse, which was being ridden with a bitless bridle for the first time, suddenly took off and she fell onto the road. There was evidence that horses may display exuberance when first ridden in a bitless

6 But if the animal was behaving in a way that may be considered docile, the claim is likely to fail under both paragraphs (a) and (b) of s.2(2). See for example *Fry v. Morgan* [2006] C.L.Y. 192, where the claimant was knocked over by a horse which the joint expert thought was probably simply being inquisitive and was not attacking him. The judge held that both paragraphs (a) and (b) were not made out. See also *Livingstone v. Armstrong* (11 December 2003, Newcastle County Court: unreported) where a motorist collided with a cow which had escaped onto a road at night. There was no evidence that the cow was displaying an abnormal characteristic for its species, it was simply standing in the road at the time of the accident, and so the claim failed on the basis that paragraph (b) had not been made out: the damage had not been caused by any abnormal characteristic of the animal.

bridle, but that this occurs in less than one per cent of horses. Two of the judges in the Court of Appeal questioned whether the second limb of paragraph (b) was satisfied on this evidence, since:

> *"A characteristic of an animal is something inherent in the animal. An unprecedented, one-off action of an animal is not a characteristic of that animal. It is difficult to say of action that occurs in less than 1 per cent of horses fitted with bitless bridles that it is characteristic of them at particular times or in particular circumstances."* [7]

The decision in *McKenny v. Foster* [2008] EWCA Civ 173 is probably best understood in this way as well, i.e. as an example of behaviour which was so exceptional that it could not properly be considered a characteristic of the animal. The facts are as bizarre as they are tragic. A cow had recently been separated from her calf. In her agitation at this separation, she escaped from an enclosed field and got onto a main road, where she collided with a car. The driver of the car was injured and her partner, who was a passenger, killed. The extent of the cow's agitation was demonstrated by the fact that, in order to escape from the field and get on to the road, she must have first jumped a six bar gate and then crossed a 12 foot cattle grid. It was not normal for a cow to behave in such an extreme way in circumstances where she was separated from her calf. Indeed this exceptional and exaggerated agitation *"was scarcely a characteristic of the cow other than possibly in the very limited sense that ... this behaviour for some reason occurred."* Paragraph (b) had therefore not been made out.[8]

---

7 See Stanley Burnton L.J. at [40], with whom Lewison L.J. at [54] agreed. But Maurice Kay L.J. at [21]-[22] considered that a characteristic had clearly been established on the evidence.

8 See May L.J. at [39]. Behaviour of this kind was also not known to the defendants and so (to the extent that it amounted to a characteristic) the requirement of knowledge under paragraph (c) was also not made out. By contrast, in *McKaskie v. Cameron* (1 July 2009, Preston County Court: unreported) liability under s.2(2) was made out where the claimant was injured when she was attacked by cows with calves at foot whilst walking with her dog through the field where they were kept. It was held that the second limb of paragraph (b) was satisfied, since (whilst it is not normal for cows to attack people) this was normal behaviour for cows in circumstances where they had calves at foot and in the presence of a dog.

What is a normal characteristic?

As explained above, both limbs of paragraph (b) require consideration of what are (or are not) "normal" characteristics for the species in question. It should also be borne in mind that s.11 of the Act provides that "species" includes sub-species and variety (which also covers breeds of animal), and so the comparison may be by reference to this smaller grouping.[9] This may be an important consideration in cases involving animals with distinct characteristics according to the breed, for example dogs, where the comparison may need to be made by reference to the particular breed rather than the species of animal in question.

The Court of Appeal considered the meaning of "normally" for the purpose of paragraph (b) in *Welsh v. Stokes* [2007] EWCA Civ 796. They noted that, depending on the context, normal can mean "conforming to type" or "usual". The former meaning was considered to be the core meaning and to equate with what is natural for an animal (while the latter meaning connotes a greater degree of regularity of frequency of occurrence than the former). The court held that, for the purpose of paragraph (b), "normally" should bear its core meaning of "conforming to type". It would therefore apply in cases where the relevant characteristic is natural, although unusual, in the animal which had caused the damage.[10] This is perhaps of greater significance in cases where the second limb of paragraph (b) is relied on. The range of behaviour which will satisfy the second limb of paragraph (b) will cover behaviour which occurs only infrequently, provided that it can be shown to be natural for the species in question.[11]

---

9 See the section dealing with the meaning of species in Chapter 3 above.

10 See Dyson L.J. (with whom the other two members of the Court of Appeal agreed) at [41]-[47].

11 But note Dyson L.J.'s comments in *Welsh v. Stokes* at [44] that even the meaning conforming to type: *"must connote some frequency of occurrence. If a characteristic is rarely found in animals of the same species, it may be difficult to say that the characteristic conforms to the type of animal in question."* It seems that this is the same point that was discussed above in relation to what amounts to a characteristic, i.e. that there must be a degree of predictability of the behaviour relied on if it is to amount to a characteristic at all. Further, the more unusual the behaviour, the more difficult it may be to satisfy the knowledge requirement under paragraph (c).

One of the difficulties that can arise in practice is to distinguish between a characteristic which is present in all animals of the same species, but to varying degrees, and one which is truly different from other animals of the same species. This is relevant to the question of whether the first limb of paragraph (b) is made out, i.e. whether or not the characteristic relied on is abnormal for the species. As we have seen, in *Wallace v. Newton* the horse was found to be unpredictable and unreliable in his behaviour, in a way that is not normally found in horses, such that the first limb of paragraph (b) was satisfied. But it is a truism that all horses (indeed all animals) can be unpredictable and unreliable in their behaviour. The question is thus when does such behaviour (for example by its frequency or severity) cross the line such that the animal has an abnormal characteristic, and in some cases there may well be a legitimate range of opinion on the point.[12]

At particular times or in particular circumstances

As we have seen, the second limb of paragraph (b) requires characteristics which are normally found in the species at particular times or in particular circumstances. It has been said that this denotes times or circumstances which can be described or predicted.[13]

As to particular times, there can of course be marked changes in animals' behaviour at certain times of the year. In *Kane v. McKenna* (1991) 1 B.N.I.L. 105 a young boy was attacked by a bantam cockerel kept by the defendant, suffering a serious injury to one of his eyes. The

12 See also *Fox v. Kohn* where the claimant alleged that the horse in question had a propensity to refuse to stop once galloping. The Court of Appeal appears to have accepted that such a characteristic would be abnormal for horses, so as to satisfy the first limb of paragraph (b). But that allegation was not made out on the evidence, and the claimant was only able to establish that the horse was difficult to stop. The trial judge's finding that this was not an abnormal characteristic was upheld by the Court of Appeal. Otton L.J. agreed that this was: "*a characteristic which was common to the species. Some horses are more difficult to stop than others; it is a matter of degree. Those which are more difficult to stop do not assume a characteristic which differentiates them from their species.*"

13 See *Freeman v. Higher Park Farm* [2008] EWCA Civ 1185 per Etherton L.J. at [43].

trial judge found that it is not a general characteristic of cockerels to launch attacks on humans, but bantam cockerels are prone to attack people in the spring, and so the second limb of paragraph (b) was satisfied.[14]

As to particular circumstances, the circumstances in which the characteristics are manifested can be either external or internal to the animal.[15] An example of an external circumstance is a dog being kept as a guard-dog (and bred and/or trained to behave in a certain way), such as the Alsatian in *Cummings v. Granger*. An example of an internal circumstance is an animal being in pain, such as the German Shepherd in *Collings v. Home Office* [2006] C.L.Y. 160 who attacked its police handler because it was in pain. The judge found that the second limb of paragraph (b) was satisfied, since being in pain was a circumstance within the meaning of the second limb and there was no basis in the Act for a distinction between external and internal factors.

Although it is necessary to identify the particular times or circumstances in which it is normal for the characteristics to be manifested, it seems clear that this does not go so far as to require the identification of exactly what provoked the relevant characteristic. This is demonstrated by *Mirvahedy*, where the exact stimulus which had so frightened the horses during the night causing them to escape was never identified. It was sufficient for the claimant to show that the relevant characteristics (i.e. to bolt, continue to flee, and ignore obstacles in their path) was normal for horses in circumstances where they are frightened.[16]

14 The case was decided under article 4(2) of the Animals (Northern Ireland) Order 1976 (equivalent to s.2(2) of the Animals Act 1971 in Northern Ireland). The evidence on which the finding under paragraph (b) was based is not identified in the brief report, but it may be that the tendency to attack in the spring was related to the breeding season. Note also that an appeal in this case was subsequently allowed: see (1992) 2 B.N.I.L. 125 (unfortunately the appeal is also only briefly reported, and it is not clear whether it related to the decision on liability).

15 See the passage from Lord Walker's speech in *Mirvahedy* at [138]-[139] quoted above.

16 See also *Bodey v. Hall* [2011] EWHC 2162 (QB) where the pony which was pulling a trap shot forwards when it was startled by something (although again it was not established that this was). It was held that this was normal behaviour in the particular circumstances where a horse is frightened by some unknown stimulus, and so the second limb of paragraph (b) was made out.

The link between paragraph (a) and paragraph (b)

Paragraph (b) provides that the likelihood of the damage or of its being severe (referring back to the damage requirements under the two limbs of paragraph (a)) must be "due to" the abnormal characteristics of the animal which satisfy paragraph (b).

In this way there is an important link between paragraph (a) and paragraph (b), and a potential trap for the unwary. For the characteristic which satisfies the damage requirement under paragraph (a) may not be an abnormal characteristic as required by paragraph (b). This reinforces the need, already mentioned above, for claimants to take care when identifying the characteristics relied on for the purpose of s.2(2); and for defendants to look carefully at the characteristics relied on, and indeed to ensure that claimants plead their case with sufficient particularity to permit this analysis.

Lord Nicholls's cow illustrates this point. It is worth quoting in full the passage in *Mirvahedy* at [46] in which he explained the need for the relevant characteristics to satisfy both paragraphs (a) and (b), and how this link may not be satisfied in the case of a mature cow:

> *"Take a large and heavy domestic animal such as a mature cow. There is a real risk that if a cow happens to stumble and fall on to someone, any damage suffered will be severe. This would satisfy requirement (a). But a cow's dangerousness in this regard may not fall within requirement (b). This dangerousness is due to a characteristic normally found in all cows at all times. The dangerousness results from their very size and weight. It is not due to a characteristic not normally found in cows "except at particular times or in particular circumstances"."*

As this example demonstrates, a permanent physical characteristic (such as an animal's size and weight, or its powerful jaw and sharp teeth) may well satisfy paragraph (a), and in particular the second limb of that paragraph. But it is unlikely to satisfy paragraph (b), since it is a normal characteristic of all animals of the species and is present at all times.

The leading case on the link between paragraphs (a) and (b) is *Clark v. Bowlt* [2006] EWCA Civ 978, in which the Court of Appeal applied *Mirvahedy* and specifically the point made by Lord Nicholls in the passage just quoted.

In *Clark* the claimant was driving his car on a public road when he came up behind the defendant who was riding her horse on the verge beside the road. As he went to pass her, the horse made a sudden uncontrolled movement into the road and collided with the side of his car. The claimant (as well as the defendant) was injured and his car was damaged. The trial judge found that the horse was a heavy animal, weighing some 600 pounds, and that because of this the second limb of paragraph (a) was satisfied, since any damage caused by the horse was likely to be severe. The judge went on to find that the second limb of paragraph (b) was also satisfied since the horse had a characteristic, described as an inclination to move otherwise than as directed, at particular times and in particular circumstances, such as when frightened by a passing car. Since the defendant had accepted she knew of the relevant characteristic, liability under s.2(2) was made out. On appeal, Lord Phillips emphasised (by reference to the example of Lord Nicholls' cow) that the characteristic which had satisfied the second limb of paragraph (a) was the horse's weight. When considering paragraph (b) the judge should have asked whether it was satisfied by this characteristic; and since the horse's weight was a normal characteristic of the species at all times, he would have been driven to conclude that paragraph (b) was not satisfied. Further, the characteristic which the judge found did satisfy paragraph (b) (if indeed it amounted to a characteristic of an animal) could not satisfy paragraph (a), and specifically the first limb of that paragraph. Horses, including this one, generally follow the direction of their rider, and so it was not likely that the horse (unless restrained) would cause this kind of damage. On the facts, the linked requirements of either limb of paragraphs (a) and (b) had therefore not been satisfied, and no liability under s.2(2) attached.

What this means in practice is that the characteristic which caused the damage, and which satisfies paragraph (a), will almost always need to be something more than just a permanent physical characteristic if it is to satisfy paragraph (b) as well. For example, in dog bite cases, it is not just the dog's powerful jaw and sharp teeth but also its propensity to attack, i.e. a behavioural characteristic. Such a behavioural characteristic may be that the dog is abnormally aggressive for its species (in which case the first limb of paragraph (b) will be satisfied), or it may be that the dog is aggressive when defending what it regards as its territory, which is a normal characteristic for dogs in those particular circumstances (in which case the second limb of paragraph (b) will be satisfied). In this way the linked requirements of paragraph (a) and paragraph (b) can both be made out.[17]

The claimant's inability to prove a behavioural characteristic explains what seems, on the face of it, the somewhat surprising outcome in *Millward v. Pritchard* (1 March 2007, Llangefni County Court: unreported), in which the claimant was injured when he was kicked by a horse. The defendant conceded that if the horse kicked someone any injury was likely to be severe, but only on the basis that this was because the horse was a large and heavy animal. The judge found that on this basis the second limb of paragraph (a) was made out. However, there was no evidence to explain the horse's behaviour (the judge rejected the claimant's account about the horse's unsettled behaviour at the time of the accident and found that it was standing still when it kicked him). Following *Clark v. Bowlt*, the judge found that the physical characteristic which satisfied paragraph (a) (i.e. its size and weight) could not satisfy paragraph (b), and so the claim under s.2(2) of the Act failed.[18]

17 It seems that the dog bite cases of *Cummings v. Granger* and *Curtis v. Betts* can be explained on this basis. But see also *Gloster v. Chief Constable of Greater Manchester* [2000] P.I.Q.R. P114, another dog bite case, where it was held that the claim failed on causation because the link between the requirements of paragraph (a) and paragraph (b) had not been made out in the unusual circumstances of that case.

18 See also the earlier case of *Whitehead v. Alexander* [2000] C.L.Y. 205 where the claimant was bitten by a horse and the claim under s.2(2) failed.

CHAPTER EIGHT KNOWLEDGE OF THE ANIMAL'S CHARACTERISTICS: S.2(2)(C) ANIMALS ACT

Introduction

Paragraph (c) of s.2(2) is concerned with the keeper's knowledge of the animal's characteristics as identified under paragraph (b). It requires either actual knowledge of the relevant characteristics on the part of the keeper, or actual knowledge on the part of another person which is imputed to the keeper in two limited situations, as explained below. The requirement of knowledge of the animal's dangerous characteristics is derived from the *scienter* action under the old common law rules, which required knowledge of the animal's propensity to cause the damage. It seems that where necessary it would be appropriate to refer back to the common law and the cases on knowledge decided under the old rules for assistance in applying paragraph (c).[1]

In practice, however, the determination of whether paragraph (c) is satisfied tends to turn more on evidential matters than on the legal interpretation of the wording of the paragraph. In this sense, paragraph (c) is rather more straightforward than the previous two paragraphs of s.2(2).

The significance of paragraph (c) as a limit on the scope of strict liability was emphasised recently in *Goldsmith v. Patchcott* [2012] EWCA Civ 183.[2] Although the policy reasons for imposing a requirement of knowledge are clear (i.e. it is because a keeper has chosen to keep an animal in the knowledge of its dangerous characteristics that he or she should be responsible for any damage which results from those characteristics), from a claimant's perspective it can sometimes seem like something of an evidential lottery. In order to prove knowledge on the

1 See *Charlesworth & Percy on Negligence (13th Ed.)* at para. 14-21 and the cases referred to at paras. 14-22 to 14-31.

2 See Jackson L.J. at [41]-[43].

part of a keeper, a claimant frequently has to rely on evidence about that knowledge which can only come directly from the keeper (i.e. the defendant) or from someone with experience of the animal in question who will often have some connection to the keeper. It may therefore be difficult for a claimant, at least at an early stage of investigation, to identify whether or not the keeper is likely to have the relevant knowledge. A potential defendant may well not volunteer evidence about this; and other witnesses may be unwilling to assist if they have still have some connection with that defendant. As mentioned in Chapter 3 above in the section dealing with the definition of a keeper, for claimants the ability to prove knowledge is an important consideration when deciding on whether to bring a claim under s.2(2) of the Act and on the identity of the defendant(s) where there is more than one keeper.

It is convenient to deal first with who must have knowledge of the relevant characteristics, before turning to consider what knowledge is required to satisfy paragraph (c).

Who must have knowledge of the characteristics?

Paragraph (c) requires that the relevant characteristics:

- Were known to the keeper; or
- Were at any time known to a person who at that time had charge of the animal as that keeper's servant; or
- Where that keeper is the head of a household, were known to another keeper of the animal who is a member of the household and under the age of sixteen.

The first of these three provisions is straightforward. It refers back to the start of s.2(2) which states that "a keeper of the animal is liable for the damage" caused by an animal. So there can be more than one keeper of an animal, and knowledge on the part of the keeper against whom the claim is brought is required.

The other two provisions allow actual knowledge on the part of someone else to be imputed to the keeper. In these two situations the keeper is fixed with knowledge, even if he or she has no actual knowledge of the relevant characteristics.

The second provision applies to someone who both (i) had charge of the animal and (ii) did so in their capacity as an employee of the keeper at the time that person acquired the knowledge of the relevant characteristics.[3] What amounts to being "in charge" of an animal is not defined in the Act, but would seem to denote an element of close control which is more than transient. The time at which the knowledge is acquired, and is imputed to the keeper, does not have to be at or immediately before the time of the claimant's injury. It seems clear that it would not matter if, by the time of the claimant's injury, the employee was no longer in charge of the animal or indeed had left the keeper's employment altogether.

The third provision applies to someone who (i) is also a keeper of the animal, (ii) is a member of the household of which the other keeper (to whom the knowledge is imputed) is the head, and (iii) is under the age of sixteen. Thus, outside this quite narrowly defined situation, relevant knowledge on the part of members of a family or household will not be imputed as a matter of law to a keeper who is a member of the same family or household, and will have to be proved. In practice, this might of course not be very difficult to prove by inference alone. Under the old common law rules there was authority for a presumption to this effect in certain circumstances, which would seem still to be applicable.[4]

North makes the point that where an animal is sold and the previous keeper parts with possession, the previous keeper will no longer have any liability under s.2(2). But the previous keeper may have knowledge

3 See *Wallace v. Newton* [1982] 1 W.L.R. 375 in which knowledge on the part of the head man in charge of the defendant's horses was imputed to the defendant (the judge also found that the defendant had actual knowledge, on the basis that it was inconceivable that her head man would have failed to tell her about the horse in question being unreliable and unpredictable in its behaviour before the claimant's accident).

4 See North, *Civil Liability for Animals* at paras. 2.119 to 2.121.

of the animal's dangerous characteristics which he or she chooses not to pass on to the new keeper. No liability can attach to the new keeper in this situation unless and until he or she acquires knowledge of those characteristics. A claimant who was injured during this time would thus have no recourse under the Act against either the previous or the new keeper.[5]

What knowledge is required?

It is clear from the wording of paragraph (c) that actual knowledge of the relevant characteristics is required. Thus a claimant cannot seek to get around any deficiency in the keeper's actual knowledge by relying on constructive knowledge (i.e. knowledge which is presumed by law on the basis that it could have been obtained with the exercise of reasonable care).[6] So it is not enough for a claimant to say that a keeper *ought* to have known of the dangerous characteristics of the animal in question.

The question of what knowledge is required to satisfy paragraph (c) is best considered by reference to whether the relevant characteristics relied on by the claimant relate to the first or the second of the two limbs of paragraph (b). As a general proposition, it is usually easier to prove knowledge of characteristics which relate to the second limb of paragraph (b) than those which relate to the first limb. This is something that claimants need to have in mind when considering how to formulate a claim under s.2(2) and specifically the characteristics relied on for the purpose of paragraph (b).

---

5 See North, *Civil Liability for Animals* at para. 2.17. The only exception would be where characteristics under the second limb of paragraph (b) are relied on, and the claimant can establish knowledge based on the new keeper's knowledge of the characteristics of the species in general (see below).

6 See *Hunt v. Wallis* [1994] P.I.Q.R. 128 per Pill J. at page 140.

Knowledge where the first limb of paragraph (b) is relied on

Where characteristics under the first limb of paragraph (b) are relied on, it is necessary to show knowledge of the animal's characteristics which are abnormal for its species in general. For example, the horse in *Flack v. Hudson* [2001] Q.B. 698 which (unlike horses generally) had a propensity to be frightened and take off when it encountered agricultural machinery. The best evidence is likely to be one or more similar incidents in which the animal has behaved in the same way and someone has been injured. It will also of course be necessary to show that the keeper was aware of the incident(s) either at the time or learnt of them prior to the subsequent incident which forms the subject of the claim. In *Flack* there had been a similar incident in which the horse took off on coming across a large agricultural machine. The defendant was present at the time, and her husband who was leading the horse was dragged and suffered a broken leg. Not surprisingly, the trial judge regarded this incident as being of "the greatest significance".

But knowledge of previous incidents which demonstrate the animal's abnormal characteristics may also be sufficient, even if these did not result in any damage. In *Wallace v. Newton* [1982] 1 W.L.R. 375 there was evidence of a number of previous incidents when the horse had shown its unpredictable and unreliable behaviour, even though it appears that no one suffered any injury as a result. Nonetheless, knowledge of these abnormal characteristics arising from the previous incidents involving the horse was sufficient to satisfy paragraph (c).

The absence of any previous incidents demonstrating the animal's abnormal characteristics (or at least any incidents of which the keeper is aware) will though be fatal where a claim is brought under the first limb of paragraph (b) (it may also present difficulties in relation to other aspects of s.2(2)). This is illustrated by *Dennett v. Wain* (18 March 2004, Preston County Court: unreported) in which the defendant's horse, which she was loose-schooling in an indoor arena, suddenly jumped over a gate to the arena and landed on the claimant, who was injured. The claimant alleged that the defendant had cracked a whip and that it was this which caused the horse to jump out of the arena, but this allegation was rejected. Having regard to the expert evidence, the judge concluded that the horse must have had an abnormal propensity to behave in this way, such that the first limb of paragraph (b) was satisfied. But there was no evidence that the horse had ever behaved in this way before. The claim under s.2(2) therefore failed because paragraph (c) was not made out.

Knowledge where the second limb of paragraph (b) is relied on

Where characteristics under the second limb of paragraph (b) are relied on, it is necessary to show knowledge of what are normal characteristics for the species at the particular times or in the particular circumstances when the damage was suffered.

This makes an important difference, as compared to a claim where characteristics under the first limb of paragraph (b) are relied on, because a claimant does not need to rely on previous incidents involving the animal (in the way outlined in the previous section) in order to prove the necessary knowledge under paragraph (c). Instead, the requirement of knowledge may be made out by showing that a keeper knows that in general animals of the species normally behave in a certain way at the particular times or in the particular circumstances when the damage was suffered.

Welsh v. Stokes [2007] EWCA Civ 796 is authority for this proposition, although knowledge was established on this basis in previous cases, including in *Mirvahedy v. Henley* [2003] UKHL 16. In *Welsh* the relevant characteristic was rearing in circumstances where the horse did not want to go forward and the rider lacked the necessary to skill to control it. The question arose about how knowledge on the part of the defendant keepers should be proved. The trial judge found that paragraph (c) was satisfied based on their knowledge, as experienced keepers of horses, of the behaviour of horses in general, i.e. that it was normal for horses to behave in this way in these particular circumstances. The Court of Appeal rejected the defendants' argument that the necessary knowledge can only be proved by showing that the keeper knew the particular animal had previously behaved in that way, and that knowledge of the behaviour of the species in general was not sufficient to satisfy paragraph (c). Dyson L.J. said this at [71]:

> *"I do not see why a keeper's knowledge that a horse has the characteristic of normally behaving in a certain way in particular circumstances cannot be established by showing that the keeper knows that horses as a species normally behave in that way in those circumstances. ... It makes no sense to require a keeper, if aware of that general characteristic, to have some additional and more particular knowledge."*

There are two important practical points that follow from this. First, a claimant can expect to find it easier to establish knowledge on this basis where a defendant is experienced in keeping animals of the species in question than where a defendant is not. As Lord Scott put it in *Mirvahedy* at [119]: *"a professional keeper of animals will have a more extensive strict liability than an ignorant amateur."* [7]

Second, there are though some limits on the assistance that this approach to proving knowledge may provide to a claimant. For the more unusual the characteristic the more difficult it may be for the claimant to establish knowledge based on a keeper's general knowledge of the species; and a defendant may say that, notwithstanding some experience with animals of the relevant species, he or she has no knowledge of the relevant characteristic. Thus in *Smith v. Harding* (26 November 2013, Manchester County Court: unreported), where the claimant was injured when the defendant's horse kicked out as she went to clip its head, the claim failed under paragraph (c). It appears that the defendant had some experience with horses but his evidence, which the judge accepted, was that he had never experienced a horse kicking out when about to be clipped. The judge made the point that, whilst it is no doubt true that all horsemen know that all horses will kick in some circumstances, that was not the test. The question was whether all horsemen know that all horses will kick out in the particular circum-

---

7 In *Mirvahedy* the defendant keepers were described as experienced horse owners and knowledge was established on this basis. See also, for example, *Goldsmith v. Patchcott* [2012] EWCA Civ 183 where knowledge was established on this basis.

stances pertaining in that case. Having accepted the defendant's evidence that he had never experienced a horse kicking out when about to be clipped, the necessary knowledge under paragraph (c) was not established.

PART THREE

DEFENCES TO STRICT LIABILITY FOR DANGEROUS ANIMALS UNDER THE ANIMALS ACT 1971

CHAPTER NINE
INTRODUCTION TO THE DEFENCES TO STRICT LIABILITY

Outline of the defences to strict liability

The chapters in Part 2 above considered the requirements for strict liability under s.2(1) and s.2(2) respectively of the Act. However, a finding that the requirements of strict liability are made out does not necessarily mean that a claimant will recover damages, either at all or in full. There are various defences which will defeat a claim based on strict liability or, in the case of contributory negligence, lead to a reduction in a claimant's damages.

The defences may conveniently be divided between (i) those provided by the Act itself (i.e. the statutory defences), and (ii) various other defences which are available in any personal injury claim. Both groups of defences apply equally to claims brought under s.2(1) and under s.2(2) of the Act.

Where the requirements of s.2(1) or s.2(2) of the Act are met, strict liability is imposed on a keeper of the animal that has caused damage, but subject to the qualification "except as otherwise provided by this Act". This qualification refers to the three statutory defences to strict liability which are provided by s.5 of the Act.

In summary, a keeper can rely on the three statutory defences to strict liability where: (i) the damage was due wholly to the claimant's own fault (s.5(1)); (ii) the claimant voluntarily accepted the risk of the damage (s.5(2)); or (iii) the claimant was a trespasser at the time he or she suffered the damage (unless the animal which caused the damage was kept for the protection of persons or property, and it was unreasonable to keep it for that purpose) (s.5(3)). Where a keeper can establish one of the statutory defences, it provides a full defence to the strict liability which would otherwise be imposed on the keeper under the Act.

So a claimant who establishes the requirements for strict liability under s.2(1) or s.2(2) of the Act, but is then met with a successful defence under s.5, will recover nothing. It is important therefore for both claimants and defendants in any case involving a claim under s.2 to go on to consider as well whether one or more of the three statutory defences may apply.

Each of the statutory defences is considered in turn in the following Chapters 10 to 12 of this part (although in practice, as we shall see, there is quite often an overlap between the defences under s.5(1) and s.5(2)). The other defences which may be relied on are then considered separately in Chapter 13, namely (i) contributory negligence and (ii) limitation. There are though a number of points of general application relating to the statutory defences which can conveniently be mentioned at the outset.

Purpose of the statutory defences

First, the purpose of the statutory defences is to provide some protection to defendant keepers (and their insurers) against the regime of strict liability. *Cummings v. Granger* [1977] Q.B. 397 is the first reported case in which the Court of Appeal had to consider a claim brought under s.2 of the Act. The Court of Appeal gave some guidance about how in general the courts should approach the statutory defences provided by the Act:

> *"That brings us straight to section 5, which is the important section providing for defences. It is important, I think, to remember that this is not a negligence action; this is not a fault liability situation; this is a strict liability situation, which is quite different. Therefore, the defences which are made available to the defendant by the statute are very important and ought not to be whittled away. To be fair to him and to be fair to the plaintiff, each of them must have their full statutory rights."*[1]

1 *Cummings v. Granger* per Ormrod L.J. at p.407.

This approach appears to have informed the Court of Appeal's subsequent decision about the application of the statutory defence in *Goldsmith v. Patchcott* [2012] EWCA Civ 183.[2] The appeal in *Goldsmith* concerned (amongst other things) the operation of s.5(2) of the Act dealing with voluntary acceptance of risk. The appellant claimant sought to avoid a finding that the defendant keeper could rely on the statutory defence by contending for a narrow construction of s.5(2) (the facts of the case are considered in more detail in Chapter 11 below). This restrictive approach was rejected by the Court of Appeal. The Court was concerned to ensure that the keeper could rely on the statutory defence in circumstances where both parties were aware of the animal's dangerous characteristics, echoing the importance of maintaining this potential "escape route" for defendants identified in the earlier passage in *Cummings* set out above. These two cases thus provide strong authority that a court should not take a restrictive approach in the application of the statutory defences.[3]

Burden of proof for the statutory defences

Second, the wording of the relevant provisions of s.5 deals only partially with the burden of proof. In s.5(3) the burden of proving the statutory defence (so far as it relates to the purpose for which the animal was kept on the premises) appears to be placed on the defendant keeper. But so far as the wording of the other two statutory defences under s.5(1) and s.5(2) are concerned, the wording of these provisions is silent about where the burden of proof lies. In practice, however, a claimant is likely to be careful to avoid, if possible, volunteering evidence which suggests that they were wholly at fault or voluntarily accepted the risk of injury. So it will almost always be incumbent on a defendant to adduce evid-

2 See in particular per Jackson L.J. in *Goldsmith* at [45]: *"Defences of this nature assume particular importance in cases of strict liability imposed by statute. This is because they provide an escape route for defendants who face tortious liability, even though their conduct was neither negligent or otherwise culpable."*

3 See also *Turnbull v. Warrener* [2012] EWCA Civ 412 per Lewison L.J. at [55] who considered that a "realistic application" of s.5(2) may restore the balance where a finding of strict liability would otherwise be made out, given the potentially wide scope of s.2(2).

ence to try to prove the statutory defences (including evidence elicited in cross-examination of the claimant and/or any witnesses called on his or her behalf).

Pleading the statutory defences

Third, while perhaps not strictly speaking required by the Civil Procedure Rules, in practice a defendant who intends to rely on any of the statutory defences would be well-advised to plead this in the Defence.[4] If nothing else, by making clear that one or more of the statutory defences is relied upon by the defendant, this ensures that the claimant then knows the case that he or she has to meet at trial and in turn has the opportunity to obtain any evidence in rebuttal.[5]

4 See C.P.R. rule 16.5 and the Practice Direction to Part 16.

5 The danger for a defendant who fails to plead reliance on a statutory defence or to adduce evidence to prove it is well illustrated by the case of *Puzey v. Wellow Trekking* (11 February 2005, Bristol County Court: unreported). The judgment records that the defence under s.5(2) was not pleaded by the defendant and neither was it raised in evidence or argument. It only surfaced in response to a question from the judge. Although it appears that the claimant was recalled at a late stage in the case to deal with the point, it does not come as a great surprise that the judge did not have any difficulty in finding that the defence under s.5(2) was not made out.

CHAPTER TEN
DAMAGE DUE WHOLLY TO THE FAULT OF THE CLAIMANT: S.5(1) ANIMALS ACT

The requirements of s.5(1)

A claim would fail under the old common law rules where a claimant was found to be solely responsible for the injury inflicted by an animal by reason of his or her own fault. This defence was retained under the Act, which provides in s.5(1) that:

> *(1) A person is not liable under sections 2 to 4A of this Act for any damage which is due wholly to the fault of the person suffering it.*

Fault in this context means the negligence, breach of statutory duty or other act or omission which gives rise to a liability in tort of the claimant.[1] But we are not concerned here with contributory negligence. The Act allows for a deduction for contributory negligence where the claimant's damage is the result *partly* of his or her own fault and partly the fault of the defendant (this is considered in Chapter 13 below). As the wording of s.5(1) makes clear, for a defendant to avoid strict liability altogether by virtue of this statutory defence a court has to find that the claimant was *wholly* responsible for the damage due to his or her own fault.

What amounts to fault on the part of a claimant will depend on the usual principles of tort law.[2] However, a common thread which runs

---

1 See s.11 of the Act which provides that "fault" in the Act has the same meaning as in the Law Reform (Contributory Negligence) Act 1945. S.4 of the 1945 Act says that "fault" means negligence, breach of statutory duty or other act or omission which gives rise to a liability in tort.

2 As noted above, essentially the same defence was available under the old common law rules, and so the cases decided under those rules would seem to remain relevant to deciding whether the statutory defence under s.5(1) is made out. A helpful commentary on the cases decided under the common law rules in this context may be found in North, *Civil Liability for Animals* at paras. 2.155 and 2.156.

through the case law relating to s.5(1) is that fault arises from some prior knowledge on the part of the claimant of the animal's dangerous characteristic which led to his or her injury (whether due to a warning given to the claimant or the claimant's own experience). In this way, there is clearly some overlap with the defence of voluntary acceptance of risk under s.5(2).[3] But, as just noted, the wording of s.5(1) makes clear that the claimant's own fault must be the sole cause of the damage in order for this statutory defence to apply. In practice, if the defence under s.5(1) is made out it is usually the case that the defence under s.5(2) is made out as well (but not necessarily the other way round).

It may be helpful to return to *Cummings v. Granger* [1977] Q.B. 397 to illustrate this point. As mentioned in previous chapters, the claimant in *Cummings* was attacked by a guard dog which was running loose in a scrap-yard next to the pub where she worked in the East End of London. She had entered the yard with a friend after work one night. The gates to the yard had a large warning on them saying "Beware of the Dog". At trial the claimant established strict liability under s.2(2) of the Act, but subject to a deduction of 50% contributory negligence as she had entered the yard knowing that there was a guard dog inside. The trial judge held that the defendant keeper of the dog could not rely on any of the statutory defences. The Court of Appeal upheld the judge's decision that the defendant could not avail himself of the statutory defence under s.5(1), since: *"the bite was not* wholly *due to the fault of the plaintiff, but only* partly *so."* But they disagreed with the judge in respect of the other statutory defences and held that the defendant could avoid strict liability by virtue of both s.5(2) and s.5(3) (the reasoning for this is considered in Chapters 11 and 12 respectively below). With regard to s.5(1), however, it is not clear who else (in addition to the claimant) could be held to blame for her injury. No finding of negligence was made against the defendant keeper (the trial judge had held him liable under the Animals Act alone, and the claimant did

3 As to claims involving child claimants, see the discussion about this in relation to the statutory defence under s.5(2) in Chapter 11 below. Similar considerations would seem to apply in relation to the statutory defence under s.5(1), if a defendant asserts that an injury to a child claimant was due wholly to the child's own fault.

not appeal the dismissal of her claim in negligence); and although the trial judge had also held that the defendant was unreasonable in keeping the dog in the yard, the Court of Appeal overturned his decision in this regard.[4] It may be that this can be explained as a matter of causation: the claimant's injury was caused in part by the dangerous characteristic of the dog (hence there was liability under s.2(2)) and in part by the negligence of the claimant (hence the deduction for contributory negligence).

More recently, the Court of Appeal considered the application of s.5(1) in *Turnbull v. Warrener* [2012] EWCA Civ 412. The facts in *Turnbull* have also been outlined in previous chapters, but in short the claimant fell whilst cantering the defendant's horse in open countryside when it suddenly bolted. The horse was being ridden with a bitless bridle for the first time, and it was accepted that this was the cause of the claimant losing control of the horse. Importantly, both the claimant and the defendant were experienced horsewomen, and both knew of the risk of losing control which eventuated. At trial, the claim in negligence failed, the judge finding that it was not negligent of the defendant to permit the claimant to ride the horse in a bitless bridle in the open, without first cantering him in an enclosed area. The claim under the Act also failed, on the basis that s.2(2) was not made out. In addition, the trial judge held that the defendant could rely on the statutory defence under s.5(1), on the basis that the accident was due wholly to the claimant's own fault in cantering the horse in the open without testing him adequately first. As the Court of Appeal pointed out, the difficulty with this finding was that the judge had also found that there was no material distinction to be drawn in relation to their respective riding experience and ability.[5] So if there was no finding of negligence against the defendant, there could also be no finding that the claimant was wholly at fault (or indeed at all), and hence the defendant could not rely

4 It is difficult to see how attributing fault to an animal can be a relevant concept in this context. But, in any event, it is hard to see how any blame could be attached to the dog in *Cummings*, since it was acting in a way that was normal for its species in the particular circumstances.

5 See Maurice Kay L.J. in *Turnbull* at [29] (with whom the other two judges agreed on this point).

on the statutory defence under s.5(1). She could however rely on the statutory defence under s.5(2), given their equivalent knowledge of the risk of riding with a bitless bridle (see further in Chapter 11 below). The case demonstrates therefore the importance of considering the respective knowledge of the parties, and the implications this can have for the application of the statutory defences under both s.5(1) and s.5(2).

Case law: examples of the application of s.5(1)

There are a number of first instance decisions involving s.5(1), which also give some helpful guidance about how the courts approach the application of this statutory defence in different factual contexts.

In *Jones v. Baldwin* (12 October 2010, Cardiff County Court: unreported) the defendant successfully relied on the statutory defence under section 5(1) in the context of a riding accident. The claimant was injured when he was kicked by another horse, belonging to the defendant, whilst competing in one of the showing classes at the Royal Welsh Show. A large number of horses were parading around the ring in front of the judges at trot and canter. There was a dispute about how the claimant came to be kicked, but the judge found that the claimant approached the other horse from behind too quickly and too close so that he came well within kicking range. This caused the other horse to kick out, which was normal behaviour for a horse in these circumstances. The claimant had little difficulty in establishing the three requirements for strict liability under s.2(2) of the Act (a separate claim in negligence against the defendant did not succeed). But the judge also found that if the claimant had ridden properly he would have been able to give the other horse a sufficiently wide berth and it would not have kicked out. Instead, the claimant had put himself in a dangerous position (as he fully appreciated) and that action, and that alone, was the catalyst for what then happened. In these circumstances, the statutory defence under s.5(1) (as well as under s.5(2)) was made out and the claim failed.

Staying with horses, in *Smith v. Harding* (26 November 2013, Manchester County Court: unreported) the claimant was kicked whilst clipping a horse belonging to the defendant. The judge accepted that the claimant had been warned several days before the accident not to clip the horse, because the horse had reacted badly when this had been attempted on a previous occasion. Despite this warning, the claimant went ahead and attempted to clip the horse, leading to her injury. Not surprisingly, having accepted this evidence the judge went on to find that the damage suffered was entirely the claimant's own fault, such that the defendant could rely on the statutory defence under s.5(1).

Another case where a claimant ignored a clear warning, this time involving a police dog, is *Dhesi v. Chief Constable of the West Midlands* [2000] Po.L.R. 120. The claimant, who had been involved in a violent incident, hid in some wasteland to avoid being caught by the police, who were pursuing him with a police dog. The trial judge accepted that, before releasing the dog once it had found the claimant's hiding place, the police handler called out twice to warn the claimant that he had a dog and the claimant should come out or he would release it. Having ignored these warnings the dog was released and the claimant was bitten during the ensuing struggle. The trial judge found that in these circumstances no blame could attach to the police handler, and that the damage suffered by the claimant was due wholly to his own fault. The Court of Appeal had little difficulty in upholding the decision that the defence under s.5(1) was made out.[6]

The statutory defence also succeeded in *Preskey v. Sutcliffe* (18 February 2013, Leeds County Court: unreported), another case involving a dog bite, but where the claimant knew of the risk of injury from his own general knowledge rather than any prior warning. The accident occurred in a pub, when the claimant tried to restrain the defendant's dog. No expert evidence was called, but all the witnesses accepted that a dog may bite in circumstances where it feels territorially challenged, as

6 See also *Nelmes v. Chief Constable of Avon and Somerset* (9 February 1993, Court of Appeal: unreported) where the claimant, in the course of being arrested, lashed out and kicked a police dog, which bit him. The trial judge's finding that the claimant was wholly to blame for this injury could not be disturbed.

had happened when the claimant tried to restrain it. Whilst this common knowledge assisted the claimant in establishing strict liability under s.2(2), it also permitted the defendant to rely on the statutory defence under s.5(1) as well as under s.5(2).

CHAPTER ELEVEN
VOLUNTARY ACCEPTANCE OF THE RISK OF DAMAGE: S.5(2) ANIMALS ACT

Introduction

In practice, it is the statutory defence of voluntary acceptance of risk under s.5(2) which is most frequently relied on by defendants to avoid strict liability under the Act. The sub-section provides that:

> *(2) A person is not liable under section 2 of this Act for any damage suffered by a person who has voluntarily accepted the risk thereof.*

A helpful summary of the approach which should be taken in relation to this statutory defence is given by Etherton L.J. in *Freeman v. Higher Park Farm* [2008] EWCA Civ 1185 at [48], who referred to what had been said previously in *Cummings v. Granger*:

> *"The words of s.5(2) are simple English, and must be given their ordinary meaning, and not be complicated by fine distinctions or by reference to the old common law doctrine of* volenti*:* Cummings v Granger *[1977] Q.B. 397, at 408 (Ormrod L.J.). What must be proved in order to show that somebody has voluntarily accepted the risk is that (1) they fully appreciated the risk, and (2) they exposed themselves to it:* Cummings *[1977] Q.B. 397 at 410 (Bridge L.J.)."*

Thus s.5(2) does not seek to import the common law defence of *volenti non fit injuria* into the Act, and hence it seems the principles and case law relating to *volenti* do not have any direct application when considering whether the statutory defence is made out. Rather, as the passage from *Freeman* makes clear, there are essentially two questions for the court to consider, namely: (i) whether the claimant had full knowledge of the risk of injury, and (ii) whether the claimant exposed him or herself to that risk.[1]

These two requirements of the statutory defence are considered in turn below. But there are two other points which it may be helpful to mention at this stage.

First, the scope of the statutory defence under s.5(2) is subject to an important qualification, in that (by virtue of s.6(5) of the Act) it cannot be relied on by a defendant where the claimant is an employee who incurs a risk incidental to his or her employment. This exception to the statutory defence is also considered separately below.

Second, the question of whether the statutory defence of voluntary acceptance of risk can be made out against a claimant who was a child at the time of the injury does not appear to have been addressed in any reported case. The question has, however, been decided in relation to the common law defence of *volenti* in *Buckpitt v. Oates* [1968] 1 All E.R. 1145. Although, as just mentioned, somewhat different principles apply in the context of *volenti*, the judge's reasoning in that case would appear to be equally valid in relation to the statutory defence under s.5(2). The judge held that there was no reason in principle why a child should be unable to appreciate and accept the risk; and that it was a question of fact in any case. But he noted that a court will always consider with great care whether a particular child claimant had the means and the knowledge and experience to appreciate fully and freely the risk and what he or she was agreeing to. As such, he observed that the defence *"is one which, like that of contributory negligence, becomes less*

---

1 The potential significance in practice of the different principles which apply to a defence of *volenti* in a negligence claim as opposed to a defence under s.5(2) to a claim for strict liability under the Act is illustrated by the decision in *Tutin v. Mary Chipperfield Promotions Ltd* (1980) 130 N.L.J. 807 (the facts in *Tutin* are set out in Chapter 4 above). The judge held that the statutory defence under s.5(2) was made out, on the basis that the claimant accepted the risk of a fall whilst riding a camel in a race. But he also held that she did not accept the risk of negligence which had caused her fall (and hence any defence of *volenti* to the claim in negligence could not have succeeded). The claimant therefore established liability in negligence, in circumstances where her alternative claim under s.2 of the Act failed as a result of the statutory defence.

likely to succeed on the facts as the age and experience of the infant diminish."[2] If this approach is followed in relation to the defence under s.5(2), a defendant would thus not be precluded from raising the statutory defence against a child claimant, but would need to consider very carefully whether on the facts the requirements of the statutory defence could be made out. This would seem to apply in particular to the knowledge requirement of the statutory defence, especially where a defendant relies on a claimant's general knowledge of the animal and activity to satisfy this requirement as discussed below.

Knowledge of the risk of injury

Actual knowledge

Dealing first with the knowledge requirement, it seems clear (by analogy with the knowledge requirement for a defendant under s.2(2)(c) of the Act) that actual knowledge of the risk of injury on the part of the claimant is required. Constructive knowledge (i.e. what the claimant ought to have known) is not applicable in this context.

The risk of injury

Difficulty sometimes arises, however, in defining the risk of injury which needs to be known by a claimant in order for the statutory defence to apply. In broad terms, it relates to the risk of injury due to the dangerous characteristics of the animal which satisfied s.2 and caused the accident. But what if the animal was known to behave in a certain way, albeit that on the occasion in question it behaved more violently than expected? This was the issue which arose in *Goldsmith v. Patchcott* [2012] EWCA Civ 183. In *Goldsmith* the claimant suffered a severe injury when the defendant's horse reared up and then bucked so violently that she was thrown to the ground, where she was struck by

2 See also the case law which acknowledges the reduced ability of a child to recognise danger and the risk of injury associated with a particular activity: for example *Tomlinson v. Congleton Borough Council* [2003] UKHL 47 per Lord Hoffmann at [46], and *Mullin v. Richards* [1998] 1 W.L.R. 1304 (standard of care to be applied to a child in a claim in negligence).

the horse's foot. The claimant accepted that she knew that a horse could buck if alarmed, but maintained that she was unaware that it could buck so violently that she would be thrown off and injured. She contended that she had not accepted the risk of injury from the sort of violent bucking that had in fact occurred. The trial judge rejected this argument, and the Court of Appeal upheld the judge's decision on this point. As mentioned in Chapter 9 above, the Court of Appeal considered that a restrictive application of the statutory defence, as contended for by the claimant, was not appropriate. Thus it is not necessary for a claimant to be aware of the precise behaviour which eventuates in order for the statutory defence under s.5(2) to apply. As Jackson L.J. explained:

> *"It is not a prerequisite of the section 5(2) defence that the claimant should foresee the precise degree of energy with which the animal will engage in its characteristic behaviour. Animals may act out of instinct or impulse and their precise behaviour cannot necessarily be predicted. ...*
>
> *If the claimant foresaw the possibility of bucking and voluntarily accepted that risk, then section 5(2) is engaged. The fact that [the horse] bucked more violently than anticipated cannot take the case outside section 5(2), so as to defeat the defendant's defence."* [3]

Relevance of the claimant's case under s.2(2)(b)

The question of whether a claimant had the requisite knowledge of the risk in question will depend on the facts of each individual case. But, in a claim under s.2(2) of the Act, how the claimant has put his or her case under paragraph (b) of the sub-section is often an important consideration in the context of s.5(2). This is because, as mentioned already, a court is concerned here with the claimant's knowledge of the dangerous characteristic which caused the injury. If the first limb of paragraph (b) applies, then knowledge of a characteristic which is abnormal for the

3 See *Goldsmith* at [50] and [59]. See also the previous decision of the Court of Appeal in *Freeman v. Higher Park Farm* [2008] EWCA Civ 1185, on which Jackson L.J. relied in reaching the decision on this point in *Goldsmith*, in particular at [50]-[51].

species is required. But if the second limb applies, then knowledge of a characteristic which is normal for the species in the particular circumstances which were present at the time of the accident is required. As explained in the Chapter 8 above, where the second limb of paragraph (b) applies, in order to prove that the *defendant* knew of the relevant characteristic (so as to satisfy the knowledge requirement of s.2(2)(c)) it will often be sufficient to show that the defendant was an experienced keeper of the type of animal, and so knew that the animal could behave in this way in the particular circumstances. But what is sauce for the goose is sauce for the gander. So, if the claimant also has some experience of the type of animal, then the claimant may well have to accept that he or she was also well aware of the risk of injury associated with the relevant characteristic, such that the requirement of knowledge under s.5(2) is made out. Thus in practice it can often be easier for a defendant to show that a claimant had sufficient knowledge for the purpose of s.5(2) where the second limb of s.2(2)(b) is relied on by a claimant (since this can be based on general knowledge of the type of animal) as opposed to the first limb of s.2(2)(b) (since this requires knowledge of the specific risk attached to the particular animal).

This point can be illustrated by reference to two cases, both involving riding accidents, in which respectively the first and second limbs of s.2(2)(b) were relied on by the claimant. In *Flack v. Hudson* [2001] 2 W.L.R. 982 the claimant's wife was killed whilst riding the defendant's horse. The facts in *Flack* are set out in Chapter 7 above, but in short the horse had an abnormal characteristic for its species, in that it had a propensity to be frightened by agricultural machinery, such that the first limb of paragraph (b) was satisfied. The defendant knew of this characteristic and strict liability under s.2(2) was made out. The trial judge also found that the claimant's wife (unlike the defendant) had no knowledge of this specific characteristic, and hence that she had not voluntarily accepted the risk of injury. On appeal, and in order to try to get around this finding, the defendant argued that the mere act of riding any horse involves a risk of injury, as the claimant's wife (who herself had some experience of riding) must have been aware when she went riding on the day of the accident, and that this was sufficient to make out the statutory defence under s.5(2). The Court of Appeal firmly rejected this argument. So it seems clear that, in order to make out the statutory defence where the first limb of paragraph (b) is relied on, proof of the claimant's knowledge of the specific risk of injury associated with the dangerous characteristic which satisfies s.2(2) is required.

By contrast, in *Turnbull v. Warrener* [2012] EWCA Civ 412 the claimant relied on the second limb of paragraph (b) (she had fallen when the defendant's horse, which she was riding with a bitless bridle, had taken off). On appeal, the Court of Appeal held (by a majority) that the claimant had not made out the requirements of strict liability under s.2(2). But the judges went on to consider whether the defendant could in any event rely on the statutory defence under s.5(2). The point was made that both the claimant and the defendant were experienced riders, who knew of the risks inherent in riding horses. In view of this general knowledge, the claimant as well as the defendant would know that on occasions a horse will not respond to its rider's instructions or will respond in a way that the rider did not intend. If this was sufficient to satisfy the requirement of knowledge on the part of the defendant so as to make out strict liability under s.2(2), then equally it should be sufficient to satisfy the requirement of knowledge on the part of the claimant so as to make out the statutory defence under s.5(2). It was said that the defendant's ability to rely on s.5(2) in that case:

> *" ... arises from the equivalence of knowledge and experience as between the parties. If Mrs Warrener's knowledge for the purpose of s.2(2)(c) is established, it is difficult to see how knowledge as an element of voluntariness on the part of Ms Turnbull for the purpose of s.5(2) can be denied. There is, on the judge's undisputed findings, a significant symmetry in this case."* [4]

It is worth noting two first instance decisions in which a claimant's general knowledge has also supported a finding of voluntary acceptance

4 See Maurice Kay L.J. at [34], and see also Lewison L.J. at [56]. The former referred as well at [31] to the factual similarities between that case and *Goldsmith*, where the s.5(2) defence had also succeeded on the basis of the claimant's knowledge of the inherent characteristics of horses in general (which was shared with the defendant).

of risk under s.5(2).[5] In another riding case, *Plum v. Berry* (5 November 2004, Preston County Court: unreported), the claimant was bucked off by the defendant's horse. The judge found that the risk of being unseated by such an event is one which any rider who is competent to canter and hack out accepts, and hence that the claim fell "squarely within s.5(2)."[6] In *Bodey v. Hall* [2011] EWHC 2162 the claimant was travelling as a groom in a pony and trap driven by the defendant when the pony suddenly shot forward, with the result that the trap tipped and the claimant was thrown out on to the ground, suffering a severe head injury. It was common ground that the pony had been spooked by some unknown stimulus which had caused it to shoot forward, and the judge found that it was normal for a horse to behave in this way in these particular circumstances such that the second limb of paragraph (b) was made out. The defendant relied on the statutory defence under s.5(2), on the basis that when the claimant accepted her invitation to travel as a groom she (the claimant) did so accepting full responsibility for her exposure to what took place. Importantly, the claimant was an experienced horsewoman, albeit that she had only limited experience of driving in a pony and trap. The judge found that she appreciated both the general risk of horses behaving unpredictably and the particular risk that a trap could tip causing injury if a horse moved rapidly away from a perceived threat. He considered that she had acquired this level of knowledge from her own wide experience of horses. The fact that the claimant had limited experience of driving in a pony and trap, and still less had never experienced a similar situation to that which occurred on the day of the accident, did not help her. The defendant was able to rely on the statutory defence of voluntary acceptance of risk, and the claim therefore failed.

5 See also *Preskey v. Sutcliffe* (18 February 2013, Leeds County Court: unreported), referred to in the context of s.5(1) in Chapter 10 above, where the claimant (as well as the defendant) accepted that in certain circumstances a dog may bite, including when it felt territorially threatened. By seeking to restrain the defendant's dog which then bit him, he was held to have voluntarily accepted the risk of this injury.

6 See [42(7)-(8)] of the judgment in *Plum v. Berry*. This passage was cited with approval by Jackson L.J. in *Goldsmith v. Patchcott* [2012] EWCA Civ 183 at [48] and by Maurice Kay L.J. in *Turnbull v. Warrener* [2012] EWCA Civ 412 at [32].

In all cases a court must determine this issue on the evidence about the claimant's knowledge. But an adult claimant who takes part in an inherently risky activity involving animals, and who suffers an injury as a result of a danger which is well known to be associated with the animal and activity, is likely therefore to face difficulty in avoiding a finding that he or she had full knowledge of the risk, at least if he or she has some relevant prior experience. In a wider context, this may be seen as reflecting the courts' policy to avoid imposing liability for injuries sustained as a result of the ordinary dangers involved in leisure activities, where individuals have chosen to take part in those activities at their own risk.[7]

Warning of the risk of injury

If a warning of the risk of injury, whether written or verbal, has been given to a claimant then this may be good evidence on which a court can make a finding of the requisite knowledge. In *Cummings v. Granger* [1977] Q.B. 397 it was noted that the claimant must have seen the notice "Beware of the Dog" on the door to the yard before she went in, and this (amongst other things) supported the finding that the claimant had full knowledge of the risk of injury when she did so. In the context of claims under s.2(1) involving animals of a dangerous species kept in a zoo or park, it seems that a suitable warning notice would be effective to avoid liability under the Act for injury caused to visitors by dangerous animals.[8] A verbal warning may also be effective. Thus in *Smith v. Harding* (26 November 2013, Manchester County Court: unreported) referred to above, the yard owner had spoken to the claimant several days before the accident and warned her not to clip the horse, because the horse had reacted badly when she had attempted to clip him on a

7 See the House of Lords' decision in *Tomlinson v. Congleton Borough Council* [2003] UKHL 47, which was referred to by Lewison L.J. in in *Turnbull v. Warrener* [2012] EWCA Civ 412 in particular at [55]. Another example of a claim in which the statutory defence under s.5(2) was made out is *Jones v. Baldwin* (12 October 2010, Cardiff County Court: unreported), where the claimant was injured whilst competing in an event at the Royal Welsh Show. The judge noted that he was struck by the claimant's evidence "in terms of relishing the risk which this exciting sport presents."

8 See North, *Civil Liability for Animals* at para. 2.134.

previous occasion. Despite this warning, the claimant went ahead and attempted to clip the horse, leading to her injury. On this basis, the judge held that the statutory defence under s.5(2) (as well as under s.5(1)) was made out.[9]

Sometimes claimants are asked to sign disclaimers before taking part in activities involving animals. In principle, it is permissible to exclude strict liability under s.2 of the Act in this way.[10] However, such disclaimers are often worded in general terms, simply acknowledging the risk of injury associated with taking part in the activity. Where a disclaimer is in these general terms, there would seem to be scope for argument about whether it is effective to fix a claimant with full knowledge of the risk which eventuates.

Protecting property

Another area of potential dispute relates to a claimant who is injured by an animal whilst taking steps to protect his or her own property, for example by intervening in a dog fight. If a claimant intervenes in such a fight to retrieve his or her own dog, and is bitten by a defendant's dog, can the defendant rely on the statutory defence, on the basis that by intervening the claimant voluntarily accepted the risk of such injury? The issue was raised but ultimately not decided in a case under the old common law rules.[11] In a negligence claim a claimant who has reason-

9 See also *Freeman v. Higher Park Farm* [2008] EWCA Civ 1185 where the claimant was warned before riding out that the horse might buck, and this was one of the reasons for the trial judge's finding (upheld on appeal) that she had voluntarily accepted the risk of injury when the horse behaved in this way.

10 On the basis that Parliament has expressly provided by s.5(2) that liability can be excluded in this way: see *Charlesworth & Percy on Negligence (13th Ed.)* at para. 4-84. The prohibition against the exclusion of liability arising in the course of business for death or personal injury under s.2 of the Unfair Contract Terms Act 1977 applies only where this results from the defendant's negligence, and so has no application to a claim for strict liability under s.2 of the Act.

11 See *Smith v. Shields* (1964) 108 S.J. 501. The Court of Appeal held that the trial judge was entitled to find that the claimant was injured before and not during the dog fight, as the defendant had alleged, and so the question whether the claimant could recover in circumstances where she was injured whilst intervening in the

ably intervened to protect property will not be held to have consented to his or her injuries or to be contributorily negligent.[12] So a claimant may argue that the same approach should be taken in a claim for strict liability under the Act, if the statutory defence under s.5(2) is relied on by a defendant in this situation.

Exposure to the risk

The second requirement of the statutory defence identified above is that a claimant, having full knowledge of the risk, exposed him or herself to the risk. This seems to require an intent on the part of a claimant to run the risk. In practice, this second requirement is rarely in issue, since it is usually accepted on the facts that the claimant intended to run the risk.

The issue did arise, however, in *Tapp v. Trustees of the Blue Cross Society* (15 May 2013, Northampton County Court: unreported). The claimant was injured when she was bitten by a horse belonging to the first defendant which was kept at the second defendant's yard. The claimant also kept horses at the yard and had gone there to check on her own horses. Before she entered the yard she saw that several horses were loose, but they did not appear to be agitated in any way. She therefore went in to the yard, but the loose horses then came up to her and one of them bit her. The defendants sought to rely on the statutory defence under s.5(2). The judge noted what Jackson L.J. had said about the operation of the statutory defence in *Goldsmith v. Patchcott* [2012] EWCA Civ 183 at [50], namely: *"If the claimant, knowing of the risk which subsequently eventuates, proceeds to engage with the animal, his or her claim under the Act will be defeated."* He considered that on the facts the claimant was not seeking to "engage" with the defendants' horses: she was simply trying to pass through the yard when the horses came up to her and she was bitten. The decision serves as a useful reminder to consider whether this second requirement is made out on the facts of each case. Whilst in many cases there may be no realistic scope for

---

fight did not need to be determined on the facts.

12 See *Charlesworth & Percy on Negligence (13th Ed.)* at para. 4-120, and also North, *Civil Liability for Animals* at para. 2.132.

dispute, there will be exceptions. For example, what about the walker who is injured by animals whilst passing through a field in which they are kept? Adopting the judge's approach in *Tapp*, it might be argued that the claimant has not engaged with the animal which injured him or her in these circumstances, and hence that the second requirement of the statutory defence is not made out.[13]

The exception for employees

As indicated above, the scope of the statutory defence under s.5(2) is qualified by s.6(5) of the Act, which provides that:

> *(5) Where a person employed as a servant by a keeper of an animal incurs a risk incidental to his employment he shall not be treated as accepting it voluntarily.*

The effect of s.6(5) is to preclude a defendant from relying on the statutory defence of voluntary acceptance of risk where a claimant is employed by a keeper of an animal which injured the claimant in the course of his or her employment. Given that those who work with animals may be expected to have a keen understanding of the risks involved, it is not hard to see how in many cases involving the statutory defence would succeed, were it not for this prohibition. This is therefore an important exception for employees.

The exception represents a change from the position under the old common law rules. It had previously been the case that strict liability for animals was severely limited as between employer and employee.[14] The Law Commission considered that this should be changed. The rationale for doing so was that the employer, as the person carrying on the activity involving dangerous animals, is in the best position to take

---

13 The statutory defence under s.5(2) failed in *McKaskie v. Cameron* (1 July 2009, Preston County Court: unreported), where the claimant was injured by cows whilst walking across open fields, albeit that it appears this was for other reasons related to the claimant's lack of knowledge (see [330]-[336] and [355] of the judgment).

14 See *Rands v. McNeil* [1955] 1 QB 253.

precautions against or to mitigate the damage which may flow from the activity (insurance being an important way of mitigating any damage suffered by an employee).[15] Whilst employees may be well aware of the risks involved with animals, they do not have any real choice but to incur those risks, in the sense that they are required to do so as part of their employment.[16] The employer, on the other hand, profits from the employee's work and can in turn use this revenue to insure against injury caused by the animals which it chooses to keep.

An employee who is expressly employed to undertake hazardous duties with animals (for example a zookeeper, or a rider who deals with difficult or unbroken horses) would seem to be in exactly the same position as any other employee for the purpose of s.5(2) and to benefit equally from the exception.[17]

The wording of s.6(5) does however require the risk incurred to be "incidental to" the claimant's employment. Thus if a claimant was injured in an incident which occurred outside the course of his or her employment, and so was not incidental to that employment, the statutory defence under s.5(2) would still be available to a defendant.

It has been pointed out already that there may be more than one keeper of an animal. The wording of s.6(5) requires that the claimant is employed by "a keeper of an animal". If a claimant is employed by one keeper but sues another keeper, it would seem to follow that he or she would have the benefit of the exception against the latter even though that other keeper is not the claimant's employer.[18]

15 See the Law Commission Report on Civil Liability for Animals (Law Com. No.13), at para. 20.

16 If an employee has acted negligently in incurring a risk, then this may of course result in his or her claim being defeated altogether by virtue of s.5(1) of the Act, or the damages being reduced for contributory negligence.

17 See North, *Civil Liability for Animals* at para. 2.137 on whether s.6(5) covers the situation where there has been an "actual" assumption of risk by an employee.

18 This point appears to have been the subject of argument in *Smith v. Harding* (26 November 2013, Manchester County Court: unreported), but ultimately did not need to be determined since the judge held that the claimant was not an employee (see [25] of the judgment and below). In this situation the defendant keeper would

It will be apparent that in this context, as in various other areas of the law, the question of employment status, and specifically whether or not a claimant is an employee, may need to be determined. This is a complex issue, with extensive case law in a number of different areas which is likely to be relevant to determining employment status in the context of s.5(2).[19] A detailed discussion of the issue is outside the scope of this book, but a brief summary of certain general points apparent from the case law may assist:

- It is generally accepted that there is no single test to determine the relationship of employer and employee.
- A "multiple factor" approach is commonly adopted, taking into account a number of different features/tests but ultimately depending on the court's assessment of the relationship between the parties as a whole.
- The nature and extent of control over the worker is an important feature (including control over the method of working and the hours worked).
- There must be mutuality of obligation for the relationship of employer and employee to exist (in the sense of a guarantee of certain work being provided to the worker and that this in turn will be performed by the worker).
- Another relevant factor is whether the worker provides the services as a business on his or her own account, or does so as part of the other's business. This includes consideration of factors such as whether the worker provides equipment, what degree of finan-

---

not have had the benefit of the claimant's employment, and so it may be said that this is inconsistent with the rationale for the exception discussed above.

19 The question of whether the claimant was an employee for the purpose of the statutory defence under s.5(2) arose in *Smith v. Harding*, which contains a helpful discussion of the law in this area. The claimant was held not to be an employee and hence the defendant was able to rely on the statutory defence which (as indicated above) was made out on the facts.

cial risk is taken by the worker, and what degree of responsibility the worker has for investment and management.

CHAPTER TWELVE DAMAGE CAUSED TO A TRESPASSER: S.5(3) ANIMALS ACT

Introduction

The statutory defence provided by s.5(3) of the Act relates to a claimant who suffers damage caused by an animal whilst trespassing. The wording of the sub-section is as follows:

> *(3) A person is not liable under section 2 of this Act for any damage caused by an animal kept on any premises or structure to a person trespassing there, if it is proved either –*
>
> *(a) that the animal was not kept there for the protection of persons or property; or*
>
> *(b) (if the animal was kept there for the protection of persons or property) that keeping it there for that purpose was not unreasonable.*

The Act does not define the meaning of a trespasser, so it would seem that the established principles about what amounts to trespass to land should apply. Thus s.5(3) comes into play when a person suffers damage caused by an animal in the course of an unjustifiable intrusion upon land in the possession of another.[1]

As noted in Chapter 9 above, it appears that the burden of proving all aspects of the statutory defence falls on a defendant, including that the claimant was a trespasser at the time he or she suffered the damage. It should be borne in mind that a defendant keeper may not be the person in possession of the property where the incident took place (for example, the owner of a horse which is on loan and kept in a field or stables belonging to someone else). In this situation, the defendant may

1 See *Clerk & Lindsell on Torts (21st Ed.)* at para. 19.01 for this definition of a trespasser, and chapter 19 of that work generally for a helpful commentary on trespass to land.

not necessarily be able to say whether or not a claimant was trespassing at the relevant time. In such a case, if there is an issue about whether or not a claimant was a trespasser, a defendant may need to obtain evidence from the person in possession of the property to deal with this point.

The Act also does not define what amounts to a "premises or structure". However, as North points out, the wording is very reminiscent of the phraseology used in the Occupiers' Liability Act 1957 and the Occupiers' Liability Act 1984. Those Acts apply to liability for injury suffered on premises which includes "any fixed or moveable structure, including any vessel, vehicle or aircraft." If this definition was applied by analogy to the Animals Act, then s.5(3) would apply where an animal was kept in a wide range of places, including a house or other building, an open space outdoors such as a garden or field, and a car or other vehicle.[2]

If a case falls within the ambit of s.5(3) as just outlined (i.e. the damage was caused by an animal kept on any premises or structure to a person trespassing there), then a defendant must go on to prove the requirement of paragraph (a) and (if applicable) paragraph (b) of s.5(3) in order to rely on the statutory defence. In practice, as we shall see, and with the important exception of dogs, it will generally be the case that a defendant will be able to rely on the statutory defence under s.5(3) if a trespasser has suffered damage in this way.

The requirement of paragraph (a)

As to paragraph (a) of s.5(3), this requires proof that the animal was not kept on the premises or structure for the protection of persons or property. Most animals which fall within s.2(2) (i.e. animals of a non-dangerous species) will, by their very nature, be such that the require-

2 See North, *Civil Liability for Animals* at para. 2.142. But see *McKaskie v. Cameron* (1 July 2009, Preston County Court: unreported) referred to above, where the claimant was injured by cows whilst walking across open fields, which the judge considered did not fall within the meaning of "premises or structure" and hence fell outside the scope of the statutory defence under s.5(3).

ment of paragraph (a) is satisfied and hence that a defendant can rely on the statutory defence. The obvious exception is a dog, which may be kept as a guard dog for the protection of persons or property. As to animals of a dangerous species to which s.2(1) applies, in this country these animals are often (though of course not exclusively) kept for public interest and enjoyment, for example animals in a zoo or a wild-life park, rather than for protection, in which case paragraph (a) is satisfied and a defendant can again rely on the statutory defence.

Whether or not an animal is kept for the protection of persons or property may not be easy to determine. This is illustrated by *Cockhill v. Muff* (17 June 1987, Court of Appeal: unreported), albeit that s.5(3) was not directly in issue on the appeal. The claimant, whose mother was looking for grazing for a goat, was injured whilst visiting the defendants' small-holding when he was attacked and bitten by their dog, a cross-bred Labrador. There was a sign at the entrance gate to the defendants' premises saying "Beware of the Dog". The first defendant, Mr Muff, had also told a police officer after the incident that the dog was there to protect his wife. However, in evidence, Mrs Muff (his wife and the other defendant) said that the dog was a pet and not a guard dog. The trial judge found that it was not a guard dog. In the Court of Appeal, Nourse L.J. observed that:

> "*... it is not inherently inconsistent to say, on the one hand, that a dog is not a guard dog but that it is a pet and, on the other, that it is there for the protection of Mrs Muff herself. Many dogs do protect their owners simply by barking at anybody who comes on to the premises.*"

The requirement of paragraph (b)

If a court finds that the animal was kept for the protection of persons or property, it is necessary then to go on to consider paragraph (b). For a defendant can still rely on the statutory defence under s.5(3) if he or she can prove that keeping the animal on the particular premises or structure for that purpose was "not unreasonable".

This was the issue relating to s.5(3) which arose in *Cummings v. Granger* [1977] Q.B. 397. As mentioned in Chapter 10 above, the trial judge held that it was unreasonable to keep an untrained dog, which was known to be ferocious, to protect (as the judge put it) a lot of old broken-down scrap motor cars in the defendant's yard at night. The Court of Appeal took a different view on this point. It seems clear from the reasons given by the judges in the Court of Appeal that it is appropriate to take into account all relevant circumstances when determining whether keeping an animal on premises for protection was "not unreasonable". It is worth mentioning some of the features which the judges identified in support of their decision, since these may be applicable in other cases.

As just noted, the trial judge had relied in support of his finding against the defendant (amongst other things) on the fact that the dog was ferocious. But, as Lord Denning M.R. put it: *"True it was a fierce dog. But why not? A gentle dog would be no good."* Lord Denning also considered there was a reasonable need to protect scrap, which was vulnerable to theft when the yard was deserted at night and at weekends. Bridge L.J. referred to the fact that the premises where the dog was kept were fully enclosed, and so no one could get in there unless they went in quite deliberately. Further, there was a clear warning "Beware of the Dog" at the gates. He endorsed North's view that whether there was a warning of the presence of the dangerous animal on the premises may be a very significant factor in assessing reasonableness.

The Guard Dogs Act 1975 was passed after the incident which gave rise to the claim in *Cummings v. Granger* (but before the appeal in that case was heard by the Court of Appeal). The Guard Dogs Act controls the keeping and use of guard dogs on certain premises (it does not, however, apply to agricultural land, to land within the curtilage of a dwelling house, and to other buildings).[3] Where a guard dog is kept on those premises it must either be under the control of a handler or it must be secured "so that it is not at liberty to go freely about the premises". A warning notice that a guard dog is present must also be

3 See s.7 of the Guard Dogs Act which defines the meaning of "premises" for the purposes of that Act.

clearly exhibited at each entrance to the premises.[4] Contravention of these requirements gives rise to a criminal offence, but the Guard Dogs Act expressly provides that it does not confer or derogate from any civil liability.[5]

Notwithstanding this latter provision, the Court of Appeal in *Cummings v. Granger* considered that the Guard Dogs Act may affect the application of the statutory defence under s.5(3) of the Animal Act. Their observations on this point are *obiter*, since the Guard Dogs Act was not in force at the relevant time. But it is worth noting that they questioned whether it would now be reasonable to keep a guard dog loose in a commercial yard at night, and hence whether the statutory defence under s.5(3) of the Act could still assist a defendant in these circumstances.[6] The position may also be different where a guard dog is kept loose on a farm or dwelling house (as mentioned above, those premises fall outside the scope of the Guard Dogs Act). Although both these statutes have been in force for many years now, there appears to be no further authority on the point. To this extent therefore the scope of the statutory defence under s.5(3) remains uncertain and is open to argument in a future case.

If a defendant is unable to rely on the statutory defence under s.5(3) of the Act for this reason, the defence of voluntary acceptance of risk by the claimant under s.5(2) might still be available.[7] But if a claimant failed to establish strict liability under s.2(2) of the Act on account of being a trespasser, he or she might still be able to bring a claim against the occupier of the premises where the animal was kept under the Occupiers' Liability Act 1984 and/or in negligence.[8]

---

4 See s.1 of the Guard Dogs Act. The proper construction of this section was decided in *Hobson v. Gledhill* [1978] 1 W.L.R. 215.

5 See s.5 of the Guard Dogs Act.

6 See Lord Denning M.R. at page 406 and Bridge L.J. at page 409 in *Cummings v. Granger*.

7 See again Lord Denning M.R. at page 406 in *Cummings v. Granger*, and the Chapter 11 above dealing with the statutory defence under s.5(2).

8 See the relevant chapters in Part 5 below dealing with common law liability.

CHAPTER THIRTEEN OTHER DEFENCES TO STRICT LIABILITY

Introduction

Under the old common law rules certain defences were (at least arguably) available to a defendant, namely (i) act of God, and (ii) act of third party. There was also a requirement that the animal should have escaped from control at the time that it caused the damage, and hence a claim could be defended on the ground that there had been no escape from control. The effect of the abolition of the old common law rules by s.1(a) of the Act, and the absence of any corresponding statutory provision in the Act, means that these defences are no longer available to a defendant.

In addition to the statutory defences under the Act which have already been considered, the defences which are available in any personal injury claim are available in the same way to a claim for personal injury brought under s.2 of the Act.[1] Two of these defences require particular mention, namely (i) contributory negligence, and (ii) limitation. These defences are considered in turn below.

Defendants sometimes plead reliance on s.1 of the Compensation Act 2006 by way of a defence to strict liability under the Act. The section provides that a court may have regard to the deterrent effect of potential liability when determining whether a defendant should have taken particular steps to meet a standard of care (thereby enshrining in statute the well-established common law principle to the same effect). However, the scope of the section relates to the standard of care required in a claim for negligence or breach of statutory duty, so it seems clear that it can have no application to a claim for strict (i.e. no fault) liability under the Act. Thus s.1 of the Compensation Act cannot provide a defence to a claim for strict liability under the Act.

1 For a commentary on these general defences see, for example, chapter 4 of *Charlesworth and Percy on Negligence (13th Ed.)* and chapter 3 of *Clerk and Lindsell on Torts (21st Ed.)*.

(i) CONTRIBUTORY NEGLIGENCE

The Act allows for a deduction for contributory negligence where strict liability is made out under s.2 but the claimant's damage is the result partly of his or her own fault.[2] Fault on the part of the claimant in this context is as defined in the Law Reform (Contributory Negligence) Act 1945 (i.e. negligence, breach of statutory duty or other act or omission which gives rise to a liability in tort).[3] Contributory negligence in a claim under the Act is thus a partial defence and permits a reduction to be made from a claimant's damages in the usual way.

Where contributory negligence is alleged, a court is therefore required to determine (i) whether there was any fault on the part of the claimant which was causative of the injury such that it is just and equitable to reduce the claimant's damages and, if so, (ii) what percentage reduction should be made from the claimant's damages.

The first point does not raise any particular issue of principle unique to the Act. The same principles as apply in other claims in tort where contributory negligence is alleged apply equally here.

The second point concerning the apportionment of liability where there is a finding of contributory negligence does however raise a particular issue in the context of the Act. In the usual way when assessing a claimant's share in the responsibility for the damage he or she has suffered, a court is required to consider both (i) the claimant's relative blameworthiness as against the defendant's failures, and (ii) the causative potency of each parties' relevant act/omission. However, in a claim under s.2 of the Act, there is no lack of care on the part of a defendant who is held strictly liable (assuming the defendant is not also found liable in negligence or some other ground involving a lack of care). So it is hard to see how a court can make an assessment of the relative blame-

2 See s.10 of the Act which provides that for the purpose of the Law Reform (Contributory Negligence) Act 1945 any damage for which a person is liable under ss. 2 to 4 of the Act shall be treated as due to his fault; and s.11 of the Act which provides that "fault" in the Act has the same meaning as in the Law Reform (Contributory Negligence) Act 1945.

3 See s.4 of the 1945 Act.

worthiness of the parties, since no blame attaches to the defendant in this situation. It appears that this issue has not yet been addressed in any reported case. It may be that a court would simply have to focus on the aspect of causative potency when apportioning liability, weighing up the relative impact of the claimant's act/omission and the dangerous behaviour of the animal.[4]

One practical issue that can arise in relation to contributory negligence concerns the wearing of helmets in activities involving horses. In *Bodey v. Hall* [2011] EWHC 2162, where the claimant suffered a head injury when she was thrown from a pony and trap, the defendant alleged contributory negligence on the basis that the claimant (as was admitted) was not wearing a riding hat at the time of the accident. This allegation was rejected, and the trial judge relied (amongst other things) on the evidence that it was not habitual to wear riding hats whilst carriage driving, and that no rules or guidance for carriage driving had been produced which recommended this. The position might well be different, however, in a case involving a fall whilst mounted on a horse, given that wearing a hat whilst riding is now almost universal in this country (the Queen being a notable exception).[5] Dealing with horses in other situations, especially where there is a particular risk of a head injury, may also reasonably require a hat to be worn.[6]

Contributory negligence applied to claims under the old common law rules relating to animals. It would seem to be appropriate in principle for a court to have regard to cases decided under those rules when

---

4 See *Reeves v. Commissioner of Police of the Metropolis* [2000] 1 A.C. 360 on the approach to apportionment in cases where there has been no lack of care by one of the parties.

5 See also rule 49 of the Highway Code which states that children under the age of 14 must wear a suitable helmet which is fastened securely whilst riding on the road, and that other riders should follow these requirements.

6 See for example the guidance on Health and Safety in Horse Riding Establishments and Livery Yards (December 2015) published by CIEH, which notes at p.33 that it is becoming accepted practice for a hard hat to be worn when dealing with horses even when not mounted.

determining what amounts to contributory negligence in a claim brought under the Act.[7]

(ii) LIMITATION

The Limitation Act 1980 applies to a claim for personal injury under s.2 of the Act and so governs whether a defence of limitation is available to a defendant in such a claim. But there is some uncertainty about which provisions of the Limitation Act 1980 apply to such a claim, and in particular about the appropriate limitation period.

The starting point is s.10 of the Act, which provides that for the purpose of the Limitation Act 1980 any damage for which a person is liable under s.2 of the Act shall be treated as due to his fault. Under s.2 of the Limitation Act the time limit for an action founded on tort (i.e. a fault based action) is six years from the date on which the cause of action accrued. But there is also the special time limit of three years for actions in respect of personal injuries provided by s.11 of the Limitation Act, and the associated discretion to exclude that time limit under s.33 of the Limitation Act. The wording of s.11(1) of the Limitation Act provides that this three year time limit applies to "any action for damages for negligence, nuisance or breach of duty" in respect of personal injuries. So is the limitation period for a claim for personal injury brought under s.2 of the Act six years or three years (with a discretion to dis-apply the limitation period in the latter case)?

The only reported case which has addressed this issue is the County Court decision in *Clarke v. Barber* [2002] C.L.Y. 464. The claimant in that case brought a claim under s.2(2) of the Act, but had issued proceedings three years and nine months after the incident when she was bitten by the defendant's dog which gave rise to the claim. The defendant raised a limitation defence, on the basis that a three year

7 A helpful commentary on the cases decided under the common law rules in this context may be found in North, *Civil Liability for Animals* at paras. 2.161 to 2.163.

limitation period under s.11 of the Limitation Act applied to the claim. The claimant argued that the limitation period was six years, because s.11 of the Limitation Act did not apply as a claim involving strict liability under the Act was not a claim based on negligence, nuisance or breach of duty. The claimant's contention was preferred, and a six year limitation period was held to apply. The judge relied on the House of Lords' decision in *Stubbings v. Webb* [1993] A.C. 498 (a claim involving a deliberate assault and based on trespass to the person) as supporting his conclusion that a claim under s.2 of the Act did not amount to a claim for breach of duty and so fell outside the scope of s.11 of the Limitation Act.

However, some years after *Clarke v. Barber* the House of Lords held in *A v. Hoare* [2008] 1 A.C. 844 that its earlier decision in *Stubbings v Webb* was wrongly decided. In view of this, the decision in *Clarke v. Barber*, which had relied on *Stubbings*, must now be treated with caution.[8] In particular, although *A v. Hoare* again involved a claim arising out of an intentional assault, the House of Lords appeared in that case to endorse the view that all causes of action which give rise to personal injuries are governed by s.11 of the Limitation Act, and hence have a three year limitation period.[9]

The short point, therefore, is that a claimant should ensure that proceedings for personal injury based on s.2 of the Act are issued within three years of the injury in order to avoid any uncertainty. But, in any case where proceedings are issued outside the three year period, a claimant may be able to invoke the statutory discretion under s.33 of the Limitation Act to dis-apply the limitation period in appropriate circumstances (assuming that the six year limitation period does not apply).

8 See also *Charlesworth & Percy on Negligence (13th Ed.)* at para. 14-52.

9 See in particular Lord Hoffmann in *A v. Hoare* at [11], referring to the earlier decision of the Court of Appeal in *Letang v. Cooper* [1965] 1 Q.B. 232 which was approved by the House of Lords.

PART FOUR

ANIMALS AND THE HIGHWAY

CHAPTER FOURTEEN INTRODUCTION TO ANIMALS AND THE HIGHWAY

When animals encounter users of a highway, whether motorists on a road or members of the public on a right of way, there is inevitably a risk of conflict. It is hardly surprising, therefore, that in practice accidents on the highway are one of the most frequently seen situations giving rise to personal injury claims involving animals.

As we have seen in previous chapters, claims arising from accidents involving animals on the highway may be brought under s.2(2) of the Animals Act where the damage was caused by the animal's dangerous behaviour.[1] But, in the absence of strict liability under the Act, there may be liability in negligence for damage caused by animals on the highway. It is important therefore in practice to consider both causes of action in this context; and indeed claims can be, and not infrequently are, founded on s.2(2) of the Act and in negligence. From a claimant's perspective, it may be wise to plead both causes of action in order to protect the claim should one or other of them fail.

The focus of this part of the book is on claims in negligence for injury caused by animals on the highway. For claims under s.2(2) of the Act reference should be made to the chapters in Part 3 above where these claims are considered: there is nothing particular about a claim under s.2(2) involving an animal on the highway as compared to any other factual context.

Indeed, in one sense, there is also nothing particular about a claim in negligence involving an animal on the highway as compared to any other situation. The ordinary principles of negligence apply to determine liability in this situation as in any other. However, it is appropriate to consider claims in negligence involving animals on the highway separately for two reasons. First, the common law relating to

1 In principle a claim could also be brought under s.2(1) of the Act, although plainly an encounter with an animal of a dangerous species on a highway is a highly unusual event in this country.

liability in negligence for animals straying on to the highway was reformed by s.8 of the Animal Act. It is important to understand the effect of s.8 of the Act on claims in negligence where the damage is caused by animals straying on to the highway. Second, although the ordinary principles of negligence apply to claims involving animals whether the animal is on the highway or in some other situation (as considered in the next chapter), there are particular features which bear on how a court may be expected to approach the determination of liability in negligence for injury caused by animals on the highway.

It is convenient to consider in turn (i) liability in negligence for animals straying on to the highway, and then (ii) liability in negligence as it relates to different users of the highway. These aspects are considered separately in Chapters 15 and 16 respectively below.

CHAPTER FIFTEEN
ANIMALS STRAYING ON TO THE HIGHWAY

Common law position before the Animals Act

In order to understand the effect of s.8 of the Animals Act, and in turn the present state of the law about animals straying on to the highway, it is necessary to put the reform in some historical context. This requires an outline of the position at common law about liability for animals straying on to the highway before the Act.

Aside from liability for damage caused by an animal with a known vicious propensity under the *scienter* principle at common law (now replaced by s.2 of the Act), a keeper of an animal owed a duty of care under the ordinary principles of negligence. Liability would therefore attach for foreseeable damage done by an animal as a result of its keeper's failure to take reasonable care. In the same year that the House of Lords gave the classic decision on liability for negligence in *Donoghue v. Stevenson* [1932] A.C. 562 it also decided a case about the duty of care owed by the keeper of an animal in *Fardon v. Harcourt-Rivington* [1932] All E.R. 81. The case involved a dog owned by the defendant which had been left in his car parked outside Selfridge's in London (the dog had broken a window, from which a glass splinter flew out into the eye of the claimant, a passing pedestrian). The claim was brought under the *scienter* principle and in negligence. On the latter point, Lord Atkin expressed the duty of care owed by the keeper of an animal as follows:

> " ... *quite apart from the liability imposed upon the owner of animals or the person having control of them by reason of knowledge of their propensities [i.e. under the* scienter *principle], there is the ordinary duty of a person to take care either that his animal or his chattel is not put to such a use as is likely to injure his neighbour - the ordinary duty to take care in the cases put upon negligence.*"[1]

1 At page 83.

However, there was an important exception to this general rule in the case of damage caused by animals straying on to the highway. The owner or occupier of land adjoining the highway from which an animal got on to the highway causing injury or damage to a user of the highway was not liable in negligence. This exception to liability for negligence was affirmed by the House of Lords in *Searle v. Wallbank* [1947] A.C. 341. The effect of the exception was that there was no duty owed by the owner or occupier of land adjoining the highway to fence or otherwise enclose the land, or to maintain and repair any fences or other enclosures that were present. In the absence of special circumstances, no duty was owed to users of the highway for straying animals.

The exception was subject to much criticism, as being out of step with modern social conditions and traffic and an unjustifiable indulgence to farmers and other landowners.[2] The Law Commission recommended the abolition of the exception.[3] This was effected by s.8 of the Act albeit, as we shall see, with some qualification. Nonetheless, this is the one aspect of the Animals Act which brought about a substantial change in the law.

s.8 of the Animals Act

The wording of s.8 of the Animals Act is as follows:

> *(1) So much of the rules of the common law relating to liability for negligence as excludes or restricts the duty which a person might owe to others to take such care as is reasonable to see that damage is not caused by animals straying on to a highway is hereby abolished.*

---

2 See for example Bridge J. in *Bativala v. West* [1970] 1 Q.B. 716 at page 724: *"Suffice it for me to say that the rule [in* Searle v. Wallbank*] is rooted in the social conditions of an earlier age when pastoral land in England was not normally fenced, and consequently straying animals on the highway were a normal hazard of the highway which any traveller on the highway had to expect and be prepared to meet. Nowadays such conditions only survive in relatively remote parts of the country; Dartmoor springs to mind as an example. Over the major part of England and Wales the relevant social conditions are vastly different."*

3 See the Law Commission report no. 13 on Civil Liability for Animals (1967).

(2) Where damage is caused by animals straying from unfenced land to a highway a person who placed them on the land shall not be regarded as having committed a breach of the duty to take care by reason only of placing them there if–

(a) the land is common land, or is land situated in an area where fencing is not customary, or is a town or village green; and

(b) he had a right to place the animals on that land.

The effect of s.8(1) of the Act is to abolish the common law exception with regard to animals straying on to the highway as described above. As a result, the duty of care owed by owners or others responsible for animals is of general application. The ordinary duty of care in negligence, as expressed by Lord Atkin in *Fardon v. Harcourt-Rivington*, applies therefore in respect of animals straying on to the highway in the same way as in any other situation involving animals.

The remainder of this chapter considers in more detail the present law relating to animals straying onto the highway. Although they involve the same general principles, it is convenient to break the topic down between claims involving (i) animals straying on to a public road, and (ii) animals on public rights of way over private land. Before looking at these two aspects, there are a number of points relating to s.8 of the Act that also need to be considered.

First, the effect of s.8(2) of the Act, which applies where damage is caused by animals straying from unfenced land on to a highway. This provides a qualification to the general rule under s.8(1) that the keeper of an animal is under a duty to take reasonable care to see that it does not stray on to a highway and cause damage. As North puts it, the effect of s.8(2) is to indicate that there is no presumption of negligence when animals stray from unfenced land.[4] Thus it seems that there must be something more than a mere failure to fence in order to impose liability in negligence for animals straying from unfenced land.[5] It should

4 See North, *Civil Liability for Animals* at para. 5-08.

5 See Sauvain, *Highway Law (5th Ed.)* at para. 7-35. For example, where an activity which gives rise to a particular risk of escape is conducted on unfenced land

though be noted that the benefit of this protection only applies where the conditions in paragraphs (a) and (b) of s.8(2) are satisfied. In particular, the unfenced land from which the animals have strayed must be common land, or land situated in an area where fencing is not customary, or a town or village green. It does not, therefore, assist a person who places animals on land, outside these areas, which is unfenced.[6]

Second, the Act does not define a highway. In the absence of a statutory definition, it seems reasonable to assume that the definition of a highway at common law applies. If so, a highway includes not just all public roads but also public rights of way across private land such as public footpaths and bridleways.[7]

Third, fencing is defined by s.11 of the Act as including *"the construction of any obstacle designed to prevent animals from straying"*. References to fencing in this context can therefore cover other types of enclosing structure such as hedges, walls, and dykes.[8] References to fencing below should be read in this way.

---

adjoining the highway, there may be liability if an animal escapes in the course of that activity. See also *Cullum v. Clarke* [1989] C.L.Y. 2546 where it was not proved that the unfenced land from which the dog escaped was common land, but the court noted that if it had been proved as such then s.8(2) of the Act would have applied and the claim would have failed on that basis.

6 See s.8(2)(a) of the Act. The other condition, under s.8(2)(b) of the Act, is that the person must have had a right to place animals on the land which is unfenced. It therefore applies both to the owner of grazing rights on common land and to a person licensed by that owner to put animals on the common (provided the rightful number is not exceeded): see *Davies v. Davies* [1975] 1 Q.B. 172. For a detailed commentary on the application of s.8(2) of the Act see North, *Civil Liability for Animals* at paras. 5.18 to 5.26.

7 For the common law definition of a highway see Sauvain, *Highway Law (5th Ed.)* at para. 1-01 ff.

8 See *Ridyard v. Owen* (16 May 1980, Court of Appeal: unreported) in which the court considered, although ultimately did not decide, whether a rough stone wall came within the definition of fencing for the purpose of s.8(2) of the Act.

Animals straying on to the road

The standard of care

The standard of care expected of those who keep animals on land adjoining a public road is well-established: they are required to take all reasonable steps to ensure the animals do not escape and foreseeably cause damage to road users.[9]

It should be emphasised that this does not impose a general duty to fence or otherwise enclose animals kept on land adjoining a road (i.e. even in areas where s.8(2) of the Act does not apply). Whether fencing is reasonably required and, if so, the standard of the fencing required will depend on all the circumstances and is a question of fact in any particular case. The point was made clearly by Megaw L.J. in *Ridyard v. Owen* (16 May 1980, Court of Appeal: unreported), who gave a helpful summary of how this question should be approached:

> *" ... section 8 [of the Animals Act 1971] does not in itself and by itself impose upon occupiers of land adjoining the highway any general duty to fence, though it may well be that, in certain cases, fencing will in fact be necessary if the occupier is to fulfil his duty to take reasonable care. The duty that rests upon the occupier who is putting animals on land from which there is the possibility that they may stray on to the highway either directly or indirectly is a duty to take reasonable care, having regard to all the circumstances. Those circumstances include all the relevant factors that commonly have to be taken into account in deciding whether somebody is in breach of a duty of care. One has to take into account what is the extent of the risk that [animals] will escape from the land on to the highway; the extent to which, if they do escape, there is danger to passing traffic involving the extent to which traffic is to be expected and the speed at which it will be expected to be travelling, and the opportunity that a driver would be likely to have to avoid being put into sudden danger. It also would include the question of the practicability and the reasonableness of remedy. If, for example, it were possible at small expense*

9 See for example *Hole v. Ross-Skinner* [2003] EWCA Civ 774 at [19] and *Wilson v. Donaldson* [2004] EWCA Civ 972 at [33].

> *to fill a gap or to make a fence, that is something which has to be taken into consideration. In considering whether there has been a breach of a duty one has to take into account all the relevant circumstances of the particular case."* [10]

A corollary of this approach is that, in areas where the land adjoining the road is unfenced, motorists are expected to keep a proper look out for straying livestock and to drive appropriately having regard to this particular risk (see Chapter 16 on highway users below).

So, a court is required in this situation to carry out the conventional balancing exercise to determine whether there has been negligence, involving general considerations such as quantification of the risk, the consequences of the risk materialising, and the cost of protecting against the risk. It will be apparent that there are a number of particular factors that need to be taken into account in this context. These include the type and nature of the animals and their number; the nature of the road and the amount of traffic using it; the location (e.g. whether an urban or a rural area); the cost and practicality of fencing or taking other steps to contain or control animals; and, where the land is fenced, the adequacy of the fencing and what steps are taken to inspect and to maintain and repair the fencing. A body of case law has built up in this country in the period since s.8 of the Act came into force and the exception in *Searle v. Wallbank* was abolished.[11] This case law gives some further guidance about how a court may be expected to approach cases of this kind although, as ever, every case will depend on its own facts. There are though a number of practical points which need to be borne in mind in this context and which it makes sense to consider first, before turning to the case law.

---

10 On the facts in that case there was no liability for an accident caused by a sheep which had strayed on to a country road bordered by rough stone walls.

11 A substantial body of case law has also built up in Canada which North suggests may provide some guidance, by analogy, about what constitutes negligence where animals stray on to the highway (the rule in *Searle v. Wallbank* has been held not to apply in many provinces in Canada): see North, *Civil Liability for Animals* at paras. 5.10 to 5.13.

Practical points

A claimant will need to identify who was responsible for an animal which has strayed on to the road and been involved in an accident, and hence who may be a defendant for a claim. This is not always straightforward. There may be more than one animal which has strayed on to the road, with different keepers; the adjoining land may not all be owned by the same person (and indeed the animal may not have escaped from the land immediately adjacent to the road, but rather have travelled from land some distance away); and responsibility for fencing on the land from which the animal has escaped may not be clear. Further, the circumstances of the animal's escape, which will be highly relevant to liability, are often not immediately apparent, and indeed are sometimes never clearly established. Early investigation of these aspects may make all the difference. If the police or other emergency services have been involved, their reports or records should be obtained, as should those of any vet who has treated the animal where this might be relevant. Criminal proceedings (see below) or an inquest in the case of a fatal accident may also help with the investigation and gathering of evidence on these aspects.

As to responsibility for an animal which has strayed on to the road and been involved in an accident, the key question is who owes a duty with regard to fencing the land from which the animal escaped. In the usual way this duty will fall on the landowner or, if the land is let, on the tenant (depending on the terms of the tenancy agreement). But the animal may be kept on the land by another person, under an agreement which may impose some duty with regard to fencing on the keeper of the animal as well.[12]

The burden of proof with regard to negligence in a case where an animal has strayed on to the road also needs to be considered. The wording of s.8(1) does not indicate where the burden of proof should

12 See *Hoskin v. Rogers* (The Times, 25 January 1985: Court of Appeal) for an example of the duty being imposed on two parties, the landowner and the keeper of the animal in question. On the particular facts of that case, which involved a "without attention" grass purchase arrangement, the keeper was found liable for the escape of the animal, but no liability attached to the landowner.

lie. However, the Court of Appeal has held that where animals have escaped on to the road due to the failure of fencing, the burden is on the defendant to show that the escape occurred without their negligence, applying the doctrine of *res ipsa loquitur*. The burden is discharged if the defendant can prove that the animal escaped despite the exercise of all reasonable care. On this basis, it is incumbent on a defendant to seek to adduce evidence to show that the fencing was adequate for its purpose and any other relevant steps that were taken to guard against the risk of escape, as well as any non-negligent reason for the escape.[13]

Where horses, cattle, sheep, goats or swine stray on to the highway their keeper is guilty of a criminal offence under s.155 of the Highways Act 1980. But this does not mean that the keeper is liable for any damage caused by the animal straying on to the highway. There is no civil remedy for a breach of this section, and so negligence must be proved.[14] The conviction can though be relied on in evidence in a negligence claim (or indeed a claim under the Animals Act) to prove the facts on which the conviction is based in the usual way.[15]

---

13 See *Upton v. John Reid Partnership* (25 March 1997, Court of Appeal: unreported). It was accepted by the defendants at first instance in *Mirvahedy v. Henley* (4 August 2000, Exeter County Court: unreported), on the basis of the decision in *Upton*, that they bore the burden of proof on the issue of negligence (which, on the evidence, they were able to discharge: see below). This approach to the burden of proof has also been adopted in Ireland, where s.2(1) of the Animals Act 1985 is in the same terms as s.8(1) of the Act: see *O'Reilly v. Lavelle* [1990] 2 I.R. 372 and *O'Shea v. Anhold and Horse and Holiday Farm Ltd* (23 October 1996, Supreme Court: unreported). But the application of the doctrine of *res ipsa loquitur* in this context is doubted in North, *Civil Liability for Animals* at para. 5-16.

14 See *Davies v. Davies* [1975] Q.B. 172 per Lord Denning M.R. at pages 177-178. The case concerned s.135 of the Highways Act 1959, which is in substantially the same terms as s.155 of the Highways Act 1980. See also *Gardner v. Wharton* (14 January 2004, Norwich County Court: unreported).

15 See s.11 of the Civil Evidence Act 1968. But since it is a strict liability offence, it does not demonstrate any fault on the part of the keeper of the straying animals. Note too that the definition of a keeper in s.155 of the Highways Act 1980 means a person who has possession of the animals in question and so does not necessarily include the owner (cf. the definition of a keeper for the purpose of the Animals Act in s.6(3) of the Act).

<u>*Case law*</u>

There are now a number of cases in which the courts have considered the standard of care required in relation to animals which have strayed on to the road. The following is a summary of the cases which it is thought are likely to be most helpful in practice.

In *Mirvahedy v. Henley*, the leading case on s.2 of the Animals Act, a claim in negligence was also pursued at first instance. Although this aspect did not feature in the subsequent appeals, it is worth noting how the trial judge dealt with the negligence claim. The facts are set out in Chapter 7 above, but in short three horses escaped at night from the defendants' field and got on to a dual carriageway, where one of them collided with the claimant's car. The judge found that the horses had escaped by breaking through a post and barbed wire fence as well as an electric fence which enclosed the field in which they were kept. The horses were normally docile, but someone or something (the exact cause could not be established) had so frightened the horses that they had panicked and in trying to flee had broken through both fences. The fact that the horses had broken out in this way did not demonstrate that the fencing was inadequate: the judge accepted the evidence of the defendant's expert that a normal fence could not be expected to withstand such an impact.[16]

The Court of Appeal did however have the opportunity to consider the duty to fence in two cases which were decided shortly after *Mirvahedy*. In the first of these cases, *Hole v. Ross Skinner* [2003] EWCA Civ 774, a number of horses had again escaped at night from the defendant's field and got on to a dual carriageway, where at last one of them collided with the claimant's car. The evidence demonstrated that at some point during the night the barbed wire fence around the field had been cut and a gate in an adjoining field left open by unknown people, and that this had allowed the horses to escape. It was accepted that the defendant was not responsible for this. The trial judge nonetheless found the defendant liable in negligence, and appeared to base this on evidence

---

16 See *Mirvahedy v. Henley* (4 August 2000, Exeter County Court: unreported), and *Mirvahedy v. Henley* [2003] UKHL 16 per Lord Scott at [80].

about the generally poor condition of the fences and gates on the defendant's land. The Court of Appeal made clear that that was inadequate evidence on which to make a finding of negligence: what mattered was the state of the fencing at the point of escape, which had been satisfactory until the actions of the intruders. The Court of Appeal also emphasised the need to prove causation: any inadequacy in the fencing at the defendant's property was not the effective cause of the horses' escape.[17]

In the second case, *Wilson v. Donaldson* [2004] EWCA Civ 972, cattle had escaped through an open gate on the defendant's farm, crossed an adjoining farm, and from there got on to the road, where they were in collision with the claimant's car. The gate which was left open was on a heavily used public footpath, and it was common ground that it had probably been left open by a walker. The trial judge held that what had in fact happened was entirely foreseeable, and that reasonable precautions could and should have been taken to avoid the gate being left open (such as a self-closing gate). The Court of Appeal upheld his decision. It was noted that the fencing on the adjoining farm was known to be in a dilapidated condition, such that the defendant's farm in effect abutted the road. The court considered that: *"in the case of a farmer whose land abuts a road [and] is crossed by a heavily used right of way, the duty of care of the farmer extends to guarding against the carelessness of person lawfully on the land, who may either be unaware of the Country Code, or through malice or oversight may leave open a gate situated across that right of way."*[18] Although this sets a relatively high standard, it seems to be founded on the well-established principle that it is reasonably foreseeable that our neighbours (in the legal sense) will not

---

17 As to the adequacy of fencing, see also *Smith v. Sudron and Coulson* (10 April 1981, Court of Appeal: unreported) in which the court observed that if a fence, though not 100% secure, is reasonably adequate to prevent the animal in question escaping, then the duty of care is likely to be fulfilled.

18 Per Potter L.J. at [34]. Contrast with the facts in *McKenny v. Foster* [2008] EWCA Civ 173, where the cow's escape from the defendant's farm was described as extraordinary (it had either jumped or clambered over a six barred livestock gate and then somehow crossed over a 12 foot cattle grid in order to escape on to the road). The claim in negligence was abandoned at first instance, and did not form part of the appeal to the Court of Appeal.

always act with proper care. The fact that the gate was on a heavily used footpath and the relatively low cost of taking precautions to prevent the gate being left open were also significant factors.

In other decisions at first instance, a riding school proprietor who organised a gymkhana on land adjacent to a busy road was held liable where a pony escaped through open gates after its rider fell off during a race. The race involved saddling up, and it was foreseeable that the saddle might slip and the rider fall, and that in turn this might cause the pony to take off.[19] There was no liability where cows had escaped from farmland enclosed by dykes and gates on to the road and collided with the claimant's car. How they escaped was not known, but it was accepted that the dykes and gates were secure and both the cattle and the gates were checked regularly.[20] In escapes from unfenced land, it has been held that there was no liability where a trained Labrador was being loaded into a car in a car park after a walk in open country, when it ran off on to a busy road some 150 yards away and collided with the claimant's car. The dog had no propensity to run off, and the exercise had taken a normal pattern.[21] There was also no liability where a pony bolted and unseated its young rider, who was accompanied by her grand-parents, and then ran a quarter of a mile before coming to a road where it collided with the claimant's car. The allegation that the pony should have been kept on a leading rein during the ride was asking too much, and the intention had been to apply a leading rein when they got closer to the road.[22]

---

19 *Bativala v. West* [1970] 1 Q.B. 716. Although the case was decided before s.8 of the Act came into force, it was decided on ordinary principles of negligence (the judge held that the exception in *Searle v. Wallbank* did not apply in the special circumstances of the case) and so should remain a valid authority.

20 *Gardner v. Wharton* (14 January 2004, Norwich County Court: unreported).

21 *Cullum v. Clarke* [1989] C.L.Y. 2546.

22 *Bennet v. Belm* [2005] C.L.Y. 189.

Animals on public rights of way over private land

Where public footpaths and other public rights of way[23] cross private land the users of the right of way will frequently encounter animals kept there by the landowner or some other person with the right to do so. To say that the animals have strayed on to the right of way is perhaps misleading: the landowner or other keeper has just as much right to keep the animals there as the member of the public has to use the right of way. However, there can be no dispute that on ordinary principles of negligence a duty is owed to lawful users of the right of way by the landowner or other keeper in respect of animals which they may encounter, i.e. a duty to take reasonable care to protect users of the public right of way from foreseeable harm.[24]

This situation gives rise to a potential conflict between the interests of the public on the one hand who wish to cross the land safely and unimpeded, and the interests of those who farm the countryside and wish to put the land to most profitable use.[25] There are particular features which bear on how a court may be expected to approach the determination of whether there is liability in negligence for injury caused by animals in this situation.

The case law suggests that it is cattle and horses that are most likely to cause injury to users of public rights of way. In the case of cattle, bulls of recognised dairy breeds should never be kept at large in fields crossed by public rights of way. Beef bulls should only be kept in this situation if accompanied by cows or heifers.[26] If a beef bull is kept in a field

23 In addition to access to private land on public rights of way, under the Countryside and Rights of Way Act 2000 the public has the right to walk on mapped access land, which includes mountain, moor, heath, down and registered common land.

24 A duty of care is also owed where a member of the public enters private land with permission. See *Lowery v. Walker* [1911] A.C. 10, and also the common duty of care owed to visitors under the Occupiers' Liability Act 1957.

25 See the concluding remarks in *McKaskie v. Cameron* (1 July 2009, Preston County Court: unreported) at [379].

26 See s.59 of the Wildlife and Countryside Act 1981. Recognised dairy breeds are Ayrshire, British Friesian, British Holstein, Dairy Shorthorn, Guernsey, Jersey and Kerry. There is no prohibition on stallions being kept in fields crossed by public

crossed by a public right of way, there is clear guidance that this should only be after careful consideration of the animal's temperament and behaviour and that it should be carefully monitored.[27] Although bulls may be the most obvious source of danger, the two most common factors in incidents involving cattle and members of the public are cows with calves and walkers with dogs.[28] The standard of care required having regard to these two features was considered in *McKaskie v. Cameron* (1 July 2009, Preston County Court: unreported), in which the claimant had been trampled by cows with calves at foot in a field which she was crossing with her dog. The judge concluded that on the particular facts of the case, liability attached to the farmer, who should have taken precautions against this foreseeable risk such as fencing off the footpath or moving the cows to another field.[29] Any previous incidents involving the animals in question which are known to a defendant will plainly be highly relevant if they show a propensity to dangerous behaviour in the presence of people or dogs.[30]

---

rights of way. But it is recognised that stallions present a risk both to walkers and riders on public rights of way: see the British Horse Society advice note on stallions, which strongly recommends that stallions are not kept in fields crossed by bridleways or byways.

27 See HSE Agriculture Information Sheet (no. 17EW) on Cattle and Public Access in England and Wales.

28 See HSE Agriculture Information Sheet (no. 17EW) above. Guidance to farmers generally is also provided by the NFU in its Business Guide (ref. 407) on Livestock and Rights of Way.

29 Liability was founded on breach of the common duty of care under the Occupiers' Liability Act 1957 (as well as under s.2(2) of the Animals Act). It has been pointed out that the 1957 Act does not apply to users of a public highway and so the decision on this point should be treated with some caution (see *Charlesworth & Percy on Negligence (13th Ed.)* at para. 14-88). However, although the claim was not brought in negligence, similar considerations would seem to apply to a claim on this basis. For a claim in negligence involving an attack by a cow with suckling calf see *Ostle v. Stapleton* [1996] C.L.Y. 4443 (the judge concluded that the evidence failed to demonstrate a known risk in the circumstances, such that the cow and calf should not to have been left in a relatively small field crossed by a well-used public footpath).

30 See for example *Birch v. Mills* [1985] C.L.Y. 3683 where there had been a similar incident involving the defendant's suckler herd of Charolais cows which had been reported to his farm manager and liability in negligence was made out. By contrast in *Miller v. Duggan* [1996] C.L.Y. 4444, where the horses which attacked the claimant were found to have a previous untarnished history of behaviour, the claim in negligence failed.

CHAPTER SIXTEEN
USERS OF THE HIGHWAY

Introduction

Animals straying on to the highway have been considered in Chapter 15 above, but animals may also be brought lawfully on to the highway by their keepers. Either way, motorists will frequently encounter animals whilst using the highway. As users of the highway, both keepers of animals and motorists owe a duty of care to other users of the highway under the ordinary principles of negligence.[1] Whether there is negligence is a question of fact in each case. But there are again particular features which bear on how a court may be expected to decide whether there is liability in negligence for injury caused by these respective classes of users. It is convenient therefore to consider each of them in turn.

Keepers of animals

As just mentioned, the duty owed by the keeper of an animal to other highway users is well-established. When determining the standard of care expected of a keeper, the location of the highway and the type and nature of the animal will plainly be important factors. As was said in *Deen v Davies* [1935] 2 K.B. 282 CA:

> *"... it has been clearly established that the owner of an animal who brings it on to the highway does owe a duty to those who are using the highway to use all reasonable care to prevent the animal damaging other parties. Reasonable care in the country may not be reasonable care in the town: reasonable care in the case of one animal may not be reasonable care in the case of another."*[2]

---

1 See for example *Carryfast v. Hack* [1981] R.T.R. 464 at page 468.

2 Per Romer L.J. at page 295. For a more detailed commentary on the various factors which may be relevant when considering whether reasonable care has been taken in this situation see North, *Civil Liability for Animals* at paras. 5.28 to 5.29.

The Highway Code contains rules about animals which are brought on to the highway.[3] The rules provide guidance in relation to horses (including safety equipment and clothing for horse and rider, and how to ride on the road) and other animals (including dogs and animals being herded). A failure to observe a provision of the Highway Code may be relied on to establish liability in negligence in the usual way.[4]

However, before bringing an animal on to the highway the keeper must consider whether it is safe to do so. In the case of horses (although the proposition would seem to apply in much the same way to other animals), it has been said that a rider may be negligent in taking a horse on to a highway if there is a reasonable risk of the horse acting in an uncontrolled way, although every case must be decided on its own facts. When making such an assessment a rider is entitled to expect that motorists would drive with ordinary care and consideration for a horse and rider, but equally the way in which it is known that ordinary people do in fact use the road must not be disregarded.[5]

It is horses and dogs which feature most prominently in the case law in this area. If a horse is being ridden properly on a highway, there is no absolute duty on a rider to prevent it from going out of control. But where this happens, this may raise a *prima facie* case of negligence, such that an adequate explanation is required from the rider in order to avoid such a finding: see *Haimes v. Watson* [1981] R.T.R. 90 CA. In that case, the horse had suddenly moved from the near side of the road towards the middle and into the path of an overtaking vehicle. The rider's explanation, that the horse shied unexpectedly such that he temporarily lost control of it, was accepted and showed no fault on the rider's part, and hence there could be no finding of negligence against him.

---

3 See rules 47 to 58 of the Highway Code.

4 See s.38(7) of the Road Traffic Act 1988. But the Highways Code is only guidance and so a failure to observe the rules of the Highways Code is not necessarily determinative of liability (a summary of the case law on this point may be found in *Clerk & Lindsell on Torts (21st Ed.)* at para. 8-191).

5 See *Carryfast v. Hack* [1981] R.T.R. 464 at page 468.

Likewise, if a dog is brought on to the highway there is a duty to take reasonable care to keep it under control.[6] But it seems that a keeper who loses control of his or her dog on a highway will face greater difficulty in avoiding a finding of negligence than a rider who loses control of a horse. This probably reflects the fact that in general it should be possible to keep a dog under control by putting it on a lead, and an expectation (at least in an urban setting) that dogs are kept on leads when on or near the highway. The type and nature of the dog in this context may be of limited relevance. Thus where a St Bernard ran off on to a busy road in London and collided with a van, its keeper was held liable for failing to put it on a lead.[7] Similarly, where a fox terrier was on a loose lead which was trailing along the ground on a London street, and became entangled in the legs of a passing pedestrian when it went to chase a cat causing her to fall, its keeper was held liable. The dog should have been held sufficiently firmly to prevent it from running away.[8]

As to animals being herded on the highway, the Highway Code advises that they should be kept under control at all times, with a person in front if possible to warn other road users. It is safer not to move animals after dark, but if doing so reflective clothing and lights should be carried. Thus where cattle were being herded along a country lane at night without proper illumination, and a driver ran into and killed the herdsman at the rear, the keeper of the cattle (as well as the motorist) was found to be negligent.[9]

Motorists

The corollary of the various hazards identified above involving animals on the highway is that the reasonably careful motorist is expected to

---

6 See *Gomberg v. Smith* [1963] 1 Q.B. CA per Holroyd Pearce L.J. at page 30, following *Deen v. Davies* above.

7 See *Gomberg v. Smith* above.

8 See *Pitcher v. Martin* [1937] 3 All E.R. 918. Liability was established both in negligence and in nuisance.

9 See *Andrews v. Watts* [1971] R.T.R. 484.

anticipate these hazards and take reasonable care to avoid them. This applies not just when encountering animals on the highway, but also when it is reasonably foreseeable that the motorist may do so. Thus where a car collided with a cow at night on an unlit rural road, the judge noted that livestock on the road is a fact of life in a rural community and considered that a motorist must take this into account and adjust his or her driving accordingly.[10] Reasonable care means the care which an ordinary skilful driver would have exercised under all the circumstances, including avoiding excessive speed, keeping a good look out, and observing traffic rules and signals and so on. As is well known, the standard expected of motorists in general by the courts is a high one, reflecting the fact that a vehicle is a potentially dangerous weapon.[11]

The Highway Code gives guidance to motorists on other road users requiring extra care, including animals and horse riders and horse-drawn vehicles. Amongst other things, the Code advises motorists to drive slowly and give plenty of room when overtaking animals, and to take great care and treat all horses as a potential hazard.[12]

The requirement for motorists both to keep a proper look out for animals on the highway and to take sufficient care when overtaking them is demonstrated by *Carryfast v. Hack* [1981] R.T.R. 464. A motorist was attempting to overtake a horse and rider, when the horse started "dancing", causing the driver to brake hard and lose control of his van. The judge found that the horse and rider had been clearly visible for several hundred yards, that the driver had failed to slow down sufficiently (he was still travelling at 25 to 30 mph at least as he went to overtake), and then failed to allow plenty of room as he went to overtake. These were described as grave errors in his driving, and had led to his loss of control of the van.[13]

---

10 See *Gardner v. Wharton* (14 January 2004, Norwich County Court: unreported).

11 See *Lunt v. Khelifa* [2002] EWCA Civ 801 per Latham L.J. at [20]. A detailed commentary on the standard of care relating to motorists and other road users may be found in *Charlesworth & Percy on Negligence (13th Ed.)* at para. 10-191 ff.

12 See rules 214 and 215 of the Highway Code.

A not infrequent hazard to confront motorists is an animal which appears suddenly in the path of their vehicle. The natural reaction is to try to avoid a collision with the animal, but this may have adverse consequences for other road users. The Court of Appeal has made clear that the correct test is the same as in any other case involving a motorist: whether the motorist acted with the reasonable care to be expected in the circumstances which took place, i.e. the emergency which confronted the motorist. It is not appropriate to approach the case along the lines of whether the motorist owed a duty to the animal or a greater duty to other road users.[14] Having said that, it is perhaps no coincidence that the bus driver who braked suddenly to avoid running over a dog was exonerated of any negligence,[15] whereas the motorist who braked suddenly to avoid a pheasant (causing the Aston Martin which was following behind to collide with her Mini) was found liable.[16]

There are of course circumstances in which both the motorist and the keeper of an animal are found liable in negligence, and an apportionment of liability needs to be made. The established factors of blameworthiness and causative effect fall to be assessed when making the apportionment. In relation to causative effect, in the context of a collision between a car and a horse and rider, the Court of Appeal acknowledged that while a car is a potentially lethal weapon (see above), a horse is also capable of doing a great deal of damage, both to its rider

---

13 See also *Burns v. Ellicot* (1969) 113 S.J. 490 as to a motorist's duty when overtaking a horse and rider.

14 See *Parkinson v. Liverpool Corporation* [1950] 1 All E.R. 367 CA. See also *Gussman v. Gratton Storey* (1968) 112 S.J. 884 CA and *Welch v. O'Leary* [1998] C.L.Y. 3911.

15 See *Parkinson v. Liverpool Corporation* above.

16 See *Gussman v. Gratton Storey* above. Salmon L.J. observed that the trial judge: *"in effect ... found that as a reasonable person [the claimant] ought to have gone on and risked killing the pheasant rather than stop and put following traffic in danger for the sake of saving the pheasant's life in the interest of whoever might hope to shoot it later. To my mind it is impossible to say that that finding cannot be justified by the evidence."*

and to other road users, if it goes out of control. The rider of a horse should not therefore be equated with a pedestrian in this context.[17]

17 See *Stoddart v. Perucca* [2011] EWCA Civ 290 per Sedley L.J. in particular at [16]-[17]. See also *Andrews v. Watts* [1971] R.T.R. 484.

PART FIVE

COMMON LAW LIABILITY FOR ANIMALS

CHAPTER SEVENTEEN INTRODUCTION TO COMMON LAW LIABILITY FOR ANIMALS

As we have seen in the previous parts of the book, the Animals Act 1971 abolished the common law rules imposing strict liability for dangerous animals (replacing them with the statutory liability under s.2 of the Act) and also the exception to liability for negligence in the case of animals straying on to the highway. But aside from these reforms, common law causes of action for damage caused by animals were not affected by the Act, at least so far as claims for personal injury are concerned.[1]

The purpose of this part of the book is to consider these other causes of action, which are all essentially tortious in nature. In practice, claims in negligence feature most frequently, but other causes of action may found a claim for damage caused by animals, namely: occupiers' liability under the Occupiers' Liability Acts 1957 and 1984, trespass to the person, and nuisance. These causes of action are all derived from the common law, although in the case of occupiers' liability the law has been amended and put on a statutory basis. Negligence is considered first in Chapter 18 below, followed by the other causes of action just mentioned in Chapter 19.

As with claims in negligence for damage caused by animals on the highway which were considered in Part 4 above, these causes of action are separate from strict liability under s.2 of the Animals Act. They may therefore permit recovery for damage caused by animals in situations where strict liability under the Act does not attach. Again, from a claimant's perspective, it may be wise to plead both causes of action in order to protect the claim should one or other of them fail.[2]

1 The reforms effected by the Animals Act in relation to the common law action of cattle trespass and in relation to livestock and dogs concern damage other than personal injury to humans, and so fall outside the scope of this book.

2 Although separate causes of action, there may nonetheless be concurrent liability, i.e. both strict liability under the Act and liability founded on a common law cause of action.

CHAPTER EIGHTEEN
NEGLIGENCE

General principles

The ordinary principles of negligence apply to a claim for damage caused by an animal. Thus, in general terms, there are four principal matters that a claimant must establish in order to make out liability in such a claim, namely that: (i) a duty of care was owed, (ii) the defendant was in breach of that duty, (iii) the breach of duty caused or materially contributed to the damage suffered by the claimant, and (iv) the damage was foreseeable (i.e. the damage was not too remote to be recoverable in law).[1]

It is the second of these matters, breach of duty, which is most often in issue in practice. It can give rise to difficult questions about the appropriate standard of care to be expected, and whether the defendant's conduct fell below that standard.[2] As has been emphasised before, whether a defendant has been negligent is a question of fact and will depend on the particular circumstances of the individual case. Nonetheless, there are particular features which bear on how a court may be expected to approach this issue in various different situations involving damage caused by animals, and in particular damage caused by dogs and by horses. Claims in negligence involving these two types of animal

1 See the summary of the law in this regard in *Whippey v. Jones* [2009] EWCA Civ 452 per Aikens L.J. at [12].

2 On the question of whether the defendant's conduct fell below the appropriate standard, S.1 of the Compensation Act 2006 may be relevant in claims for damage caused by animals. The section provides that, when considering a claim in negligence or breach of statutory duty, a court may have regard to the deterrent effect of potential liability when determining whether a defendant should have taken particular steps to meet a standard of care. The effect of s.1 of the 2006 Act is to enshrine in statute the well-established common law principle to the same effect. While the provision does not, therefore, add anything to the existing common law, it does nonetheless direct a court to consider the impact of liability on a desirable activity. Since some activities involving animals may amount to a desirable activity, this is a factor that may need to be taken into account when determining whether there has been a breach of duty in a claim involving animals.

are considered separately below. Before doing so, there are several general points relating to claims in negligence for damage caused by animals which it is convenient to deal with at this stage.

On the issue of breach of duty, the courts have emphasised the importance of foreseeability of injury in determining whether a defendant has been negligent. Thus, in *Whippey v. Jones* [2009] EWCA Civ 452 it was said that:

> *"The question of whether a person has acted negligently is not answered simply by analysing what he did or did not do in the circumstances that prevailed at the time in question and then testing it against an objective standard of "reasonable behaviour". Before holding that a person's standard of care has fallen below the objective standard expected and so finding that he acted negligently, the court must be satisfied that a reasonable person in the position of the defendant (i.e. the person who caused the incident) would contemplate that injury is likely to follow from his acts or omissions. Nor is the remote possibility of injury enough; there must be a sufficient probability of injury to lead a reasonable person (in the position of the defendant) to anticipate it."* [3]

Even before the Animals Act, it was well established that the keeper of an animal was under a duty in negligence with regard to control of the animal, quite apart from any liability under the old common law rules relating to dangerous animals. This was expressed as a duty not to put or permit the animal to be in such a position where the keeper could reasonably foresee that it might cause damage. It reflected the ordinary duty not to put a chattel (or allow it to be put) to such a use as is likely to injure one's neighbour. In this sense an animal was no different from any other chattel, although it was noted that the fact that an animal is animate and capable of spontaneous action has a bearing on whether there is a breach of the duty owed by its keeper.[4]

---

3 Per Aikens L.J. at [16]. See also *Addis v. Campbell* [2011] EWCA Civ 906 at [19].

4 See *Draper v. Hodder* [1972] 2 Q.B. 556 CA, in which the earlier case law on the duty of care relating to animals was set out in detail.

A claim for damage caused by a failure to keep proper control of an animal may therefore be brought in negligence, as well as on the basis of strict liability under what is now s.2 of the Act. However, in practice a cause of action in negligence may not add anything to a claim under s.2 of the Act, at least where the damage results from a failure to control the animal. This point was made in *Whippey v. Jones*, in which the defendant's Great Dane, which had been let off the lead in a public park, knocked in to the claimant, who fell over and was injured. At trial the claim under s.2(2) of the Act failed, but liability in negligence was made out. The finding of negligence was overturned on appeal. It was noted in the Court of Appeal that: *"before holding that a person's standard of care has fallen below the objective standard expected and so finding that he acted negligently, the court must be satisfied that a reasonable person in the position of the defendant (i.e. the person who caused the incident) would contemplate that injury is likely to follow from his acts or omissions."* In this respect the test for liability in negligence was akin to that under s.2(2)(a) of the Act, and specifically the requirement under the first limb of paragraph (a) that the damage was of a kind which the animal, unless restrained, was likely to cause. Having found that the requirement for strict liability under s.2(2)(a) was not satisfied, the trial judge could not then properly go on to make a finding that negligence was made out in the alternative.[5]

Although *Whippey v. Jones* demonstrates a limitation in the scope of liability in negligence for damage caused by an animal over and above that provided by the Act, it should not be thought that it means the cause of action in negligence is no longer of any importance in practice in cases involving damage caused by an animal. Liability in negligence can still attach where a claim under the Act has failed, in circumstances where the injury results from a failure to control the animal.[6] Further,

5 See per Aikens L.J. at [16] and [20]-[21].

6 An example of this is *Smith v. Prendergast* The Times, 18 October 1984 CA where negligence was made out on the basis of the defendant's lack of knowledge of the dangerous characteristics of a stray dog he had taken in, such that he should have kept the dog tied up (it was not in dispute on the appeal that the defendant was not liable under s.2(2) of the Act as he could not satisfy the knowledge requirement in paragraph (c)). Alternatively, if injury is caused by a permanent characteristic of an animal such as its size and weight then liability may not attach

there are other situations in which a duty of care is owed with regard to risks associated with animals which requires something other than a duty to control. Again, liability in negligence can attach in these situations where a claim under the Act would not succeed (see below for examples of such cases involving dogs and horses).

Just as the ordinary principles of negligence apply to what a claimant must establish in order to succeed in a claim for damage caused by an animal, so too a defendant may rely on the ordinary defences to liability in negligence.[7] The defence of agreement to run the risk (*volenti non fit injuria*) is frequently pleaded by defendants in claims of this kind. It is important to bear in mind that the defence of *volenti* requires proof that both (i) the claimant knew of the danger created by the defendant's negligence, and (ii) the claimant agreed (either expressly or by implication) to exempt the defendant from liability for any damage suffered as a result of that danger materialising. Thus the risk that the claimant is agreeing to run is that of the defendant's negligence (i.e. not just the risk of injury). Understood on this basis, the requirements of the defence of *volenti* present a high hurdle for a defendant to overcome.[8] It should also be borne in mind that the requirements of the defence of *volenti* are different from what is required to make out the statutory defence of voluntary of acceptance of risk under s.5(2) of the Animals Act 1971.[9] Thus the statutory defence of voluntary acceptance of risk

under s.2(2) of the Act, on the basis that paragraph (b) is not satisfied (see Lord Nicholls' example of the mature cow which falls on someone in *Mirvahedy v. Henley* [2003] UKHL 16 at [46]); but there may nonetheless be a reasonably foreseeable risk of injury in this situation, such that there would be liability in negligence for any failure to take reasonable steps to guard against the risk of injury. It may also be that the person who owes a duty to control the animal is not a keeper of the animal within the meaning of the Act, such that no liability can attach to that person under s.2 of the Act (for example the organiser of a public show involving animals).

7 A detailed commentary on the defences to a claim in negligence may be found in chapter 4 of *Charlesworth & Percy on Negligence (13th Ed.)*.

8 See *Charlesworth & Percy on Negligence (13th Ed.)* at para. 4-122.

9 See *Cummings v. Granger* [1977] Q.B. 397 per Ormrod L.J. at p.408, and see also Chapter 11 above in relation to the statutory defence under s.5(2) of the Animals Act.

may provide a good defence to a claim for strict liability under s.2 of the Act in circumstances where a defence of *volenti* to a claim in negligence would not.

Dogs

Injuries involving dogs commonly occur when dogs are brought in to a public place. In *Mason v. Weeks* (10 March 1995, Court of Appeal: unreported), the Court of Appeal approved the trial judge's approach to determining whether there is negligence in this situation, which was expressed as follows:

> *"Anyone who takes a dog into a public place owes a duty of care to the public to take reasonable steps to prevent that dog causing injury. The degree of care and diligence depends on different factors: (1) the extent to which the dog had exhibited aggressive behaviour in the past; (2) size, strength and capacity of the dog to injure; (3) the particular circumstances in which the dog is coming into contact with the public."*

On the facts in that case liability in negligence was made out.[10] The defendant had taken his large Rottweiler to a busy shopping centre. The dog was on a lead but not muzzled. The claimant, who was five years old, approached the dog at a time when the defendant was talking to a friend and was not aware of his approach. The dog attacked the claimant, who was badly bitten. The Court of Appeal upheld the trial judge's finding that the defendant's inattention to his dog in the circumstances, even though it was held on a lead, fell below the standard to be expected. It is clear that in requiring a relatively high degree of diligence on the part of the defendant the court put particular weight on the type of dog, and the fact that there had been a previous incident of aggression in a shopping area.[11]

---

10 A claim based on strict liability under the Animals Act had also been made by the claimant, but this failed at trial and was not in issue on the appeal (the basis on which the claim under the Act was dismissed at trial is not explained in the judgments in the Court of Appeal).

Where dogs are allowed off the lead in a public place, for example when being walked in a park or on a public footpath, evidence about the dog's previous behaviour, in particular when encountering other people in this situation, is likely to be an important factor. Thus in a number of cases where large dogs have collided with members of the public whilst off the lead, the absence of previous similar incidents has been central to the finding that there was no negligence, on the basis that the likelihood of injury in this way was not sufficient to require a keeper to take any steps to guard against it.[12]

It is not just positive knowledge about a dog's previous behaviour which may be relevant when considering whether there has been a breach of duty. Where a defendant had taken in a stray Alsatian which three weeks later attacked a young girl who was walking past his yard, the defendant's lack of knowledge of the dog's history and behaviour was central to the finding of negligence against him. The Court of Appeal upheld the trial judge's decision that the dog could not safely be left uncontrolled until such time as the defendant had taken sufficient steps to observe and train it so that he could be confident that it could be left loose safely in these circumstances.[13]

It is also worth noting that in *Draper v. Hodder* [1972] 2 Q.B. 556 CA liability was established, despite there being no evidence of any similar previous incidents involving the dogs in question. The defendant was a breeder of Jack Russell terriers, who kept a number of puppies in an unenclosed area at his property. The dogs got out and attacked the claimant who lived nearby. The question was whether the defendant should reasonably have foreseen the risk of such an attack, and hence should have kept the dogs properly enclosed. In the absence of previous incidents, the claimant relied on expert evidence about the behaviour of

---

11 See also *Kite v. Napp* (The Times, 1 June 1982: Court of Appeal) as an example of another case in which previous known incidents of aggression involving the defendant's dog were central to the finding of negligence against the defendant (in *Kite v. Napp* strict liability under the Animals Act was also made out).

12 See *Welsh v. Brady* [2008] CSOH 45, *Whippey v. Jones* above, and *Addis v. Campbell* above.

13 See *Smith v. Prendergast* above.

the breed, and in particular the risk of aggressive behaviour when dogs of the breed are kept in a pack or group. The Court of Appeal upheld the judge's finding that the defendant knew or ought to have known of the risk of an attack in these circumstances, and that liability in negligence was made out. It is clear that the fact that the defendant was an experienced keeper of the breed was an important factor. Whether the same approach would succeed in a case where the keeper's experience of the particular breed (or of dogs in general) was much more limited must be open to doubt.

Some dogs such as Alsatians may of course be trained to bite, for either legitimate or illegitimate purposes. Not surprisingly, the courts require a high standard of care on the part of those who keep such dogs, including the police and security firms.[14] The Guard Dogs Act 1975 imposes requirements about the control of guard dogs in certain circumstances.[15] Although a civil right of action is expressly excluded by the Act,[16] it would seem that a failure to comply with the requirements of the Act could be relied on as evidence of negligence where injury is caused by a guard dog.

Horses

Like dogs, horses which are not tethered can cause damage. This seems to occur most frequently when horses get on to the highway and collide with vehicles. Claims in negligence in this situation were considered in Part 4 above, although under the law as it now stands the same general principles apply to a claim in negligence where a horse is loose and causes damage in other circumstances. Horses can also cause injury whilst being handled, for example by kicking and biting. A duty of care is owed by those who keep horses, both private individuals and those running a business, to members of the public and where relevant to employees. If appropriate precautions are not taken to guard against

14 See *Gloster v. Chief Constable of Greater Manchester Police* [2000] P.I.Q.R. P114 per Pill L.J. at page 120.

15 See s.1 of the Guard Dogs Act 1975.

16 See s.5(2) of the Guard Dogs Act 1975.

these risks, then liability in negligence may attach. Again, the ordinary principles of negligence will apply, including those relating to employer's liability where a member of staff is injured in the course of his or her employment.[17]

Unlike most other animals, however, horses are ridden and it is in this area especially that particular considerations relating to horses arise. One of the most common situations in which allegations of negligence are made is when a rider suffers an injury whilst under the instruction or supervision of another: for example, during a lesson at a riding school, or during an escorted hack or trek. There can be no dispute that (aside from any contractual relationship) a duty of care is owed to the rider by the party responsible for providing this service. The service will often include other elements, such as providing a horse to ride, protective equipment, and the facilities of a riding arena or similar. What care is reasonably required by the party providing the service will depend on many factors including the exact nature of the service itself, and the age and experience of the rider. But, as a starting point, reasonable care in this context includes making a proper assessment of the skill and experience of the rider, providing a suitable horse (both size and temperament), and providing competent instruction or supervision. In practice, parties often seek to rely on equine/equestrian expert evidence to address the standard of care; and courts are generally prepared to allow parties to do so, at least where the cost of such evidence is proportionate.

The need to take these sorts of precautions of course reflects the fact that riding is a risk sport.[18] In the context of such an activity, riders can suffer injury as a result of an accident pure and simple, without negli-

---

17 There are a range of publications providing guidance about health and safety and good practice in this context, which may assist a court when determining whether there has been a breach of duty. For example, Health and Safety in Horse Riding Establishments and Livery Yards (pub. CIEH), Health and Safety in Horse Riding Establishments (pub. HSE), and the various safety leaflets published by the British Horse Society. Equine/equestrian expert evidence may also assist on this issue.

18 For a helpful analysis of some of the issues arising in claims in negligence for injury suffered whilst taking part in a risk sport see Norris "The duty of care owed by instructors in a sporting context" [2010] J.P.I.L. 183.

gence on anyone's part. This is a conclusion that judges not infrequently reach in cases of this nature. Claimants need, therefore, to consider carefully the allegations of negligence that are made and the evidence available to support them. The position has been neatly summed up as follows:

> *"Riding, particularly riding in open country, is not risk free. Of course, an instructor must take steps to reduce the risk to what is reasonable and acceptable ... but I find that [the claimant's accident] was just that: an accident. Riders do sometimes fall from horses, even during riding lessons, it does not follow that the reason for their fall can always be identified, still less that the riding instructor is to blame."* [19]

It is not just those providing instruction or supervision in a business context who may be liable in negligence for injury suffered by a rider. As mentioned above, private individuals who keep horses can also owe a duty of care, for example when they permit someone else to ride their horse. Such a situation arose in *Harris v. Miller* [2016] EWHC 2438 where the defendant, who had recently bought a thoroughbred racehorse, allowed the claimant who was aged 14 at the time to ride the horse in an open field. The claimant, whose previous experience was limited to riding ponies, lost control of the horse, and as a result fell off and was severely injured. The judge held that in this situation:

> *"The Defendant's standard of care must be assessed by reference to that of the ordinary and reasonably prudent horse owner. Such a person would ensure that he or she is possessed of sufficient information about both horse and rider to be able to assess any risk from what is an inherently dangerous activity."* [20]

---

19 See *MacClancy v. Carenza* [2007] EWHC 479 at [75]. The judge held that an experienced and competent riding instructor needed to be aware of anything that might unexpectedly present a challenge to a nervous rider, and to foresee and guard against presenting such a rider with that situation. However, on the evidence, the claimant's case that there was a dangerous overhanging branch that caused her to fall and about which she should have been warned in advance by the instructor was not made out.

20 At [150]. The judge found that the defendant should have known that the horse would be difficult to manage for a rider such as the claimant, and that she should not have allowed the claimant to ride the horse in an open field for the first time. It was reasonably foreseeable that the claimant could lose control of the horse and be unseated in these circumstances, leading to injury of some sort (it was immaterial that the serious injury which the claimant in fact suffered may not have been foreseen). Liability in negligence was therefore made out.

CHAPTER NINETEEN
OTHER CAUSES OF ACTION

(i) OCCUPIERS' LIABILITY

The Occupiers' Liability Act 1957 regulates the duty which an occupier of premises owes to his or her visitors in respect of dangers due to the state of the premises or to things done or omitted to be done on them. Although there is limited authority on the point, it seems that this imposes a duty on an occupier in respect of the risk of injury to a lawful visitor from an animal kept on the premises.[1]

On this basis, the duty owed by an occupier is the common duty of care as provided in s.2(2) of the 1957 Act, namely a duty to take such care as in all the circumstances of the case is reasonable to see that the visitor will be reasonably safe in using the premises. There can be situations in which an occupier of premises, where an animal is kept, is not a keeper of the animal for the purpose of the Animals Act 1971 (i.e. because the animal is neither owned by the occupier nor is it in his or her possession). As with negligence considered in Chapter 18 above, there may also be situations in which the requirements for strict liability under s.2 of the Act are not made out but nonetheless a claim against an occupier for damage caused by an animal on his or her premises could succeed.[2]

---

1 See *Chauhan v. Paul* (19 February 1998, Court of Appeal: unreported). See also *Hill v. Lovett* 1992 S.L.T. 994 (a decision in Scotland under the Occupiers' Liability (Scotland) Act 1960, which is in similar terms to the Occupiers' Liability Act 1957), and North, *Civil Liability for Animals* at para. 5-08. With regard to the duty owed by an occupier to trespassers see the Occupiers' Liability Act 1984.

2 In *Chauhan v. Paul* above, where the defendant occupiers' dog had chased the claimant postman, causing him to fall as he ran away, the trial judge found that there was no evidence to give them reason to believe that the dog had the propensity to chase visitors to their premises. The Court of Appeal held that this finding was fatal to the claimant's case both under s.2(2) of the Animals Act (in particular the knowledge requirement under paragraph (c)) and under the Occupiers' Liability Act 1957 (as the risk of injury was not reasonably foreseeable).

(ii) TRESPASS TO THE PERSON

Where an animal is used intentionally to inflict injury on someone, the injured person has a cause of action for trespass to the person (strictly speaking the tort of battery). The fact that the injury was caused through the agency of an animal is not material.[3]

However, the cause of action is not made out where the infliction of force was lawful. Claims based on trespass to the person for injury caused by an animal seem to be brought most frequently by claimants who have been bitten by police dogs. The police (and indeed any person) have a defence to such a claim where the infliction of force can be justified under s.3(1) of the Criminal Law Act 1967. This provides that a person may use such force as is reasonable in the circumstances in the prevention of crime, or in effecting or assisting in the lawful arrest of offenders or suspected offenders or of persons unlawfully at large. The issue which then has to be determined (amongst others) is whether the use of force by the release of a dog was reasonable in the circumstances.[4]

(iii) NUISANCE

Nuisance has been defined as an act or omission which is an interference with, disturbance of or annoyance to, a person in the exercise or enjoyment of (i) a right belonging to him or her as a member of the public (i.e. a public nuisance), or (ii) his or her ownership or occupation of land (i.e. a private nuisance).[5]

---

3 See *Gloster v. Chief Constable of Greater Manchester Police* [2000] P.I.Q.R. P114 per Pill L.J. at page 120, and *Roberts v. Chief Constable of Kent* [2008] EWCA Civ 1588 per Aikens L.J. at [21]. Where an animal is injured by another animal there is a cause of action against the owner of the animal which inflicted the injury for trespass to goods, if the owner has intentionally caused the act complained of: see *Manton v. Brocklebank* [1923] 2 K.B. 212 CA per Atkin L.J. at page 229.

4 See *Pollard v. Chief Constable of West Yorkshire Police* [1999] P.I.Q.R. P219, and *Roberts v. Chief Constable of Kent* above for decisions on this issue.

5 See *Clerk & Lindsell on Torts (21st Ed.)* at para. 20-01, and see generally chapter 20 of *Clerk & Lindsell* on nuisance.

In relation to animals, there can be an actionable public nuisance where an animal is unlawfully in a public place, and a private individual suffers particular damage over and above the general inconvenience and injury suffered by the public. Thus a dog running loose in the street which causes injury to a member of the public has been held to give rise to liability in nuisance (as well as in negligence) on the part of is owner.[6] As to private nuisance, this can arise where an animal on one area of land unduly interferes with a neighbour's comfortable and convenient enjoyment of his or her land.

There is an important distinction however between public and private nuisance with regard to personal injury, since as the law presently stands damages are recoverable for personal injury in a claim founded on public nuisance, but it is extremely doubtful whether damages are recoverable for personal injury in a claim founded on private nuisance. But, in distinction to negligence, an injunction is available as a remedy in a claim in nuisance. Thus in *Clarkson v. Bransford* [1987] C.L.Y. 1166, where the defendant kept 24 snakes in his attic, one of which escaped and was found by a neighbour in the cylinder cupboard of his house, an injunction was granted restraining the defendant from keeping snakes at his property.[7]

---

6 See *Pitcher v. Martin* [1937] 3 All E.R. 918.

7 The claim was brought in negligence and nuisance, which were admitted by the defendant. The claimant developed a neurosis about snakes and, in addition to the granting of an injunction, he recovered damages for this psychiatric damage.

APPENDIX
THE ANIMALS ACT 1971

Strict liability for damage done by animals

1 New provisions as to strict liability for damage done by animals.

(1) The provisions of sections 2 to 5 of this Act replace—

(a) the rules of the common law imposing a strict liability in tort for damage done by an animal on the ground that the animal is regarded as ferae naturae or that its vicious or mischievous propensities are known or presumed to be known;

(b) subsections (1) and (2) of section 1 of the Dogs Act 1906 as amended by the Dogs (Amendment) Act 1928 (injury to cattle or poultry); and

(c) the rules of the common law imposing a liability for cattle trespass.

(2) Expressions used in those sections shall be interpreted in accordance with the provisions of section 6 (as well as those of section 11) of this Act.

2 Liability for damage done by dangerous animals.

(1) Where any damage is caused by an animal which belongs to a dangerous species, any person who is a keeper of the animal is liable for the damage, except as otherwise provided by this Act.

(2) Where damage is caused by an animal which does not belong to a dangerous species, a keeper of the animal is liable for the damage, except as otherwise provided by this Act, if—

(a) the damage is of a kind which the animal, unless restrained, was likely to cause or which, if caused by the animal, was likely to be severe; and

(b) the likelihood of the damage or of its being severe was due to characteristics of the animal which are not normally found in animals of the same species or are not normally so found except at particular times or in particular circumstances; and

(c) those characteristics were known to that keeper or were at any time known to a person who at that time had charge of the animal as that keeper's servant or, where that keeper is the head of a household, were known to another keeper of the animal who is a member of that household and under the age of sixteen.

3 Liability for injury done by dogs to livestock.

Where a dog causes damage by killing or injuring livestock, any person who is a keeper of the dog is liable for the damage, except as otherwise provided by this Act.

4 Liability for damage and expenses due to trespassing livestock.

(1) Where livestock belonging to any person strays on to land in the ownership or occupation of another and—

(a) damage is done by the livestock to the land or to any property on it which is in the ownership or possession of the other person; or

(b) any expenses are reasonably incurred by that other person in keeping the livestock while it cannot be restored to the person to whom it belongs or while it is detained in pursuance of section 7 of this Act, or in ascertaining to whom it belongs;

the person to whom the livestock belongs is liable for the damage or expenses, except as otherwise provided by this Act.

(2) For the purposes of this section any livestock belongs to the person in whose possession it is.

(3) This section does not apply in relation to horses on land in England (as to which, see section 4A).

4A Liability for damage and expenses due to horses on land in England without lawful authority

(1) This section applies where a horse is on any land in England without lawful authority.

(2) The person to whom the horse belongs is liable for—

(a) any damage done by the horse to—

(i) the land, or

(ii) any property on it which is in the ownership or possession of the freeholder or occupier of the land, and

(b) any expenses which are reasonably incurred by a person detaining the horse under section 7A or 7B of this Act—

(i) in keeping the horse while it cannot be restored to the person to whom it belongs or while it is detained under section 7A or 7B of this Act, or

(ii) in ascertaining to whom it belongs.

This is subject to the other provisions of this Act.

(3) For the purposes of this section a horse belongs to the person in whose possession it is.

5 Exceptions from liability under sections 2 to 4A.

(1) A person is not liable under sections 2 to 4A of this Act for any damage which is due wholly to the fault of the person suffering it.

(2) A person is not liable under section 2 of this Act for any damage suffered by a person who has voluntarily accepted the risk thereof.

(3) A person is not liable under section 2 of this Act for any damage caused by an animal kept on any premises or structure to a person trespassing there, if it is proved either—

(a) that the animal was not kept there for the protection of persons or property; or

(b) (if the animal was kept there for the protection of persons or property) that keeping it there for that purpose was not unreasonable.

(4) A person is not liable under section 3 of this Act if the livestock was killed or injured on land on to which it had strayed and either the dog belonged to the occupier or its presence on the land was authorised by the occupier.

(5) A person is not liable under section 4 of this Act where the livestock strayed from a highway and its presence there was a lawful use of the highway.

(5A) A person is not liable under section 4A of this Act in respect of a horse which strays from a highway when its presence there was a lawful use of the highway.

(6) In determining whether any liability for damage under section 4 of this Act, or under section 4A of this Act so far as relating to a straying horse in England, is excluded by subsection (1) of this section the damage shall not be treated as due to the fault of the person suffering it by reason only that he could have prevented it by fencing; but a person is not liable under that section where it is proved that the straying of the livestock on to the land would not have occurred but for a breach by any other person, being a person having an interest in the land, of a duty to fence.

6 Interpretation of certain expressions used in sections 2 to 5.

(1) The following provisions apply to the interpretation of sections 2 to 5 of this Act.

(2) A dangerous species is a species—

(a) which is not commonly domesticated in the British Islands; and

(b) whose fully grown animals normally have such characteristics that they are likely, unless restrained, to cause severe damage or that any damage they may cause is likely to be severe.

(3) Subject to subsection (4) of this section, a person is a keeper of an animal if—

(a) he owns the animal or has it in his possession; or

(b) he is the head of a household of which a member under the age of sixteen owns the animal or has it in his possession;

and if at any time an animal ceases to be owned by or to be in the possession of a person, any person who immediately before that time was a keeper thereof by virtue of the preceding provisions of this subsection continues to be a keeper of the animal until another person becomes a keeper thereof by virtue of those provisions.

(4) Where an animal is taken into and kept in possession for the purpose of preventing it from causing damage or of restoring it to its owner, a person is not a keeper of it by virtue only of that possession.

(5) Where a person employed as a servant by a keeper of an animal incurs a risk incidental to his employment he shall not be treated as accepting it voluntarily.

Detention and sale of trespassing livestock

7 Detention and sale of trespassing livestock.

(1) The right to seize and detain any animal by way of distress damage feasant is hereby abolished.

(2) Where any livestock strays on to any land and is not then under the control of any person the occupier of the land may detain it, subject to subsection (3) of this section, unless ordered to return it by a court.

(3) Where any livestock is detained in pursuance of this section the right to detain it ceases—

(a) at the end of a period of forty-eight hours, unless within that period notice of the detention has been given to the officer in charge of a police station and also, if the person detaining the livestock knows to whom it belongs, to that person; or

(b) when such amount is tendered to the person detaining the livestock as is sufficient to satisfy any claim he may have under section 4 of this Act in respect of the livestock; or

(c) if he has no such claim, when the livestock is claimed by a person entitled to its possession.

(4) Where livestock has been detained in pursuance of this section for a period of not less than fourteen days the person detaining it may sell it at a market or by public auction, unless proceedings are then pending for the return of the livestock or for any claim under section 4 of this Act in respect of it.

(5) Where any livestock is sold in the exercise of the right conferred by this section and the proceeds of the sale, less the costs thereof and any costs incurred in connection with it, exceed the amount of any claim under section 4 of this Act which the vendor had in respect of the livestock, the excess shall be recoverable from him by the person who would be entitled to the possession of the livestock but for the sale.

(6) A person detaining any livestock in pursuance of this section is liable for any damage caused to it by a failure to treat it with reasonable care and supply it with adequate food and water while it is so detained.

(7) References in this section to a claim under section 4 of this Act in respect of any livestock do not include any claim under that section for damage done by or expenses incurred in respect of the livestock before the straying in connection with which it is detained under this section.

(8) Subsections (2) to (7) do not apply to horses on land in England (as to which, see sections 7A to 7C).

7A Power of local authorities in England to detain horses

(1) A local authority in England may detain a horse which is in any public place in its area, if the conditions in subsection (2) are met.

(2) The conditions are—

(a) the local authority has reasonable grounds for believing that the horse is there without lawful authority, and

(b) if the land is lawfully occupied by a person—

(i) that person consents to the detention of the horse, or

(ii) the local authority has reasonable grounds for believing that that person would consent to the detention of the horse (but this does not require the authority to seek consent).

(3) Section 7C contains further provision about detention under this section.

(4) In this section "local authority" means—

(a) a county council,

(b) a district council,

(c) a London borough council,

(d) the Common Council of the City of London, and

(e) the Council of the Isles of Scilly.

7B Powers of freeholders and occupiers in England to detain horses

(1) This section applies where a horse is on any land in England without lawful authority.

(2) The horse may be detained—

(a) in any case, by the occupier of the land, and

(b) if the freeholder is not the occupier, by the freeholder with the occupier's consent.

(3) Section 7C contains further provision about detention under this section.

7C Detention of horses under sections 7A and 7B

(1) This section applies where a horse is detained under section 7A or 7B.

(2) The right to detain the horse ceases at the end of the period of 24 hours beginning with the time when it is first detained unless, within that period, the person detaining the horse gives notice of the detention to—

(a) the officer in charge of a police station, and

(b) if the person detaining the horse knows to whom the horse belongs, that person.

(3) Where notice is given under subsection (2), the right to detain the horse ceases if, within the period of 96 hours beginning with the time when it is first detained, the person entitled to possession of the horse—

(a) claims it, and

(b) complies with the condition in subsection (4).

(4) The condition is that the person tenders to each person with a claim under section 4A in respect of the horse such amount as is sufficient to satisfy the claim.

(5) If by the end of the 96 hour period referred to in subsection (3) the right to detain the horse has not ceased under this section—

(a) ownership of the horse passes to the person detaining the horse, and

(b) accordingly, the person detaining the horse may dispose of it by selling it, arranging for it to be destroyed or in any other way.

(6) Where a horse is sold under this section and the proceeds of sale, less the costs of the sale and any costs incurred in connection with it, exceed the amount of any claims under section 4A in respect of the horse, the excess is recoverable from the person detaining the horse by the person who would have been entitled to possession of the horse but for this section.

(7) A person detaining a horse under this section is liable for any damage caused to it by a failure to treat it with reasonable care and supply it with adequate food and water while it is so detained.

(8) References in this section to a claim under section 4A in respect of any horse do not include a claim under that section for damage done by or expenses incurred in respect of the horse before it was on the land without lawful authority.

(9) In calculating a period of 96 hours for the purposes of this section, disregard any time falling on—

(a) a Saturday or Sunday,

(b) Good Friday or Christmas Day, or

(c) a day which is a bank holiday in England and Wales under the Banking and Financial Dealings Act 1971.

Animals straying on to highway

8 Duty to take care to prevent damage from animals straying on to the highway.

(1) So much of the rules of the common law relating to liability for negligence as excludes or restricts the duty which a person might owe to

others to take such care as is reasonable to see that damage is not caused by animals straying on to a highway is hereby abolished.

(2) Where damage is caused by animals straying from unfenced land to a highway a person who placed them on the land shall not be regarded as having committed a breach of the duty to take care by reason only of placing them there if—

(a) the land is common land, or is land situated in an area where fencing is not customary, or is a town or village green; and

(b) he had a right to place the animals on that land.

Protection of livestock against dogs

9 Killing of or injury to dogs worrying livestock.

(1) In any civil proceedings against a person (in this section referred to as the defendant) for killing or causing injury to a dog it shall be a defence to prove—

(a) that the defendant acted for the protection of any livestock and was a person entitled to act for the protection of that livestock; and

(b) that within forty-eight hours of the killing or injury notice thereof was given by the defendant to the officer in charge of a police station.

(2) For the purposes of this section a person is entitled to act for the protection of any livestock if, and only if—

(a) the livestock or the land on which it is belongs to him or to any person under whose express or implied authority he is acting; and

(b) the circumstances are not such that liability for killing or causing injury to the livestock would be excluded by section 5(4) of this Act.

(3) Subject to subsection (4) of this section, a person killing or causing injury to a dog shall be deemed for the purposes of this section to act for the protection of any livestock if, and only if, either—

(a) the dog is worrying or is about to worry the livestock and there are no other reasonable means of ending or preventing the worrying; or

(b) the dog has been worrying livestock, has not left the vicinity and is not under the control of any person and there are no practicable means of ascertaining to whom it belongs.

(4) For the purposes of this section the condition stated in either of the paragraphs of the preceding subsection shall be deemed to have been satisfied if the defendant believed that it was satisfied and had reasonable ground for that belief.

(5) For the purposes of this section—

(a) an animal belongs to any person if he owns it or has it in his possession; and

(b) land belongs to any person if he is the occupier thereof.

Supplemental

10 Application of certain enactments to liability under sections 2 to 4A.

For the purposes of the Fatal Accidents Acts 1846 to 1959, the Law Reform (Contributory Negligence) Act 1945 and the Limitation Act 1980 any damage for which a person is liable under sections 2 to 4A of this Act shall be treated as due to his fault.

11 General interpretation.

In this Act—

"common land" means—

(a) land registered as common land in a register of common land kept under Part 1 of the Commons Act 2006;

(b) land to which Part 1 of that Act does not apply and which is subject to rights of common within the meaning of that Act;

"town or village green" means land registered as a town or village green in a register of town or village greens kept under Part 1 of the Commons Act 2006;

"damage" includes the death of, or injury to, any person (including any disease and any impairment of physical or mental condition);

"fault" has the same meaning as in the Law Reform (Contributory Negligence) Act 1945;

"fencing" includes the construction of any obstacle designed to prevent animals from straying;

"horse" includes an ass, mule or hinny;

"livestock" means cattle, horses, sheep, pigs, goats and poultry, and also deer not in the wild state and, in sections 3 and 9, also, while in captivity, pheasants, partridges and grouse;

"poultry" means the domestic varieties of the following, that is to say, fowls, turkeys, geese, ducks, guinea-fowls, pigeons, peacocks and quails;

"public place" includes—

(a) any common land or town or village green;

(b) any highway (and the verges of any highway); and

"species" includes sub-species and variety.

12 Application to Crown.

(1) This Act binds the Crown, but nothing in this section shall authorise proceedings to be brought against Her Majesty in her private capacity.

(2) Section 38(3) of the Crown Proceedings Act 1947 (interpretation of references to Her Majesty in her private capacity) shall apply as if this section were contained in that Act.

13 Short title, repeal, commencement and extent.

(1) This Act may be cited as the Animals Act 1971.

(2) The following are hereby repealed, that is to say—

(a) in the Dogs Act 1906, subsections (1) to (3) of section 1; and

(b) in section 1(1) of the Dogs (Amendment) Act 1928 the words "in both places where that word occurs".

(3) This Act shall come into operation on 1st October 1971.

(4) This Act does not extend to Scotland or to Northern Ireland.

Source: http://www.legislation.gov.uk/ukpga/1971/22
(annotations removed)

'The Law of Driverless Cars: An Introduction' by Alex Glassbrook
'A Practical Guide to Costs in Personal Injury Cases' by Matthew Hoe
'A Practical Guide to Alternative Dispute Resolution in Personal Injury Claims – Getting the Most Out of ADR Post-Jackson' by Peter Causton, Nichola Evans, James Arrowsmith
'A Practical Guide to Personal Injuries in Sport' by Adam Walker & Patricia Leonard
'A Practical Guide to Marketing for Lawyers' by Catherine Bailey & Jennet Ingram
'The No Nonsense Solicitors' Practice: A Guide To Running Your Firm' by Bettina Brueggemann
'Baby Steps: A Guide to Maternity Leave and Maternity Pay' by Leah Waller
'The Queen's Counsel Lawyer's Omnibus: 20 Years of Cartoons from the Times 1993-2013' by Alex Steuart Williams

www.ingramcontent.com/pod-product-compliance
Lightning Source LLC
LaVergne TN
LVHW022042200926
848481LV00003B/753